PHYSICIANS FOR HUMAN RIGHTS

Physicians for Human Rights (PHR) mobilizes the health professions and enlists support from the general public to protect and promote the human rights of all people. PHR believes that human rights are essential preconditions for the health and well-being of all members of the human family.

Since 1986, PHR members have worked to stop torture, disappearances, and political killings by governments and opposition groups; to improve health and sanitary conditions in prisons and detention centers; to investigate the physical and psychological consequences of violations of humanitarian law in internal and international conflicts; to defend medical neutrality and the right of civilians and combatants to receive medical care during times of war; to protect health professionals who are victims of violations of human rights; and to prevent medical complicity in torture and other abuses.

As one of the original steering committee members of the International Campaign to Ban Landmines, PHR shared the 1997 Nobel Peace Prize, awarded to the Campaign and its coordinator, Jody Williams. PHR currently serves as co-chair of the US Campaign to Ban Landmines.

The President is Charles Clements, M.D.; Vice President is Carola Eisenberg, M.D. The Executive Director is Leonard S. Rubenstein, J.D.; Deputy Director is Susannah Sirkin; Advocacy Director is Holly Burkhalter; Senior Program Associate is Richard Sollom; Director of Communications is Barbara Ayotte; Director of Finance & Administration is Lori Maida; Development Coordinator is Steve Brown; Campaign and Education Coordinator is Gina Cummings; and Media Relations Coordinator is Caitriona Palmer. William Haglund, Ph.D., is Director of the International Forensic Program and Senior Medical Consultant is Vincent Iacopino, M.D., Ph.D.

Physicians for Human Rights
100 Boylston Street, Suite 702
Boston, MA 02116
Tel. (617) 695-0041
Fax. (617) 695-0307
E-mail: phrusa@phrusa.org
http://www.phrusa.org

Physicians for Human Rights
110 Maryland Ave., NE, Suite 511
Washington, DC 20002
Tel. (202) 547-9881
Fax. (202) 547-9050

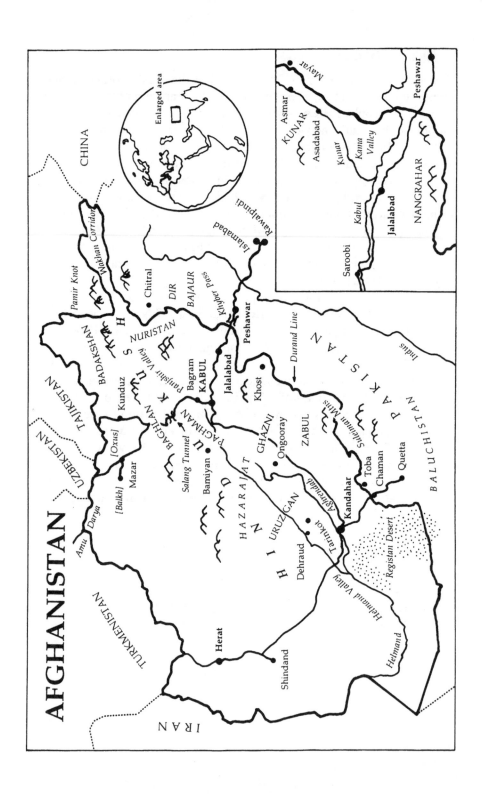

THE TALIBAN'S WAR ON WOMEN

A Health and Human Rights Crisis in Afghanistan

A REPORT BY
PHYSICIANS FOR HUMAN RIGHTS

BOSTON • WASHINGTON DC

CONTENTS

ACKNOWLEDGMENTS

This report was written by Vincent Iacopino, M.D., Ph.D., Senior Medical Consultant to Physicians for Human Rights (PHR), Boston, MA; Zohra Rasekh, M.P.H., a Senior Health Researcher for PHR; Alicia Ely Yamin, J.D., M.P.H., Assistant Professor of Clinical Public Health and Staff Attorney for the Law and Policy Project, Columbia University School of Public Health; Lynn Freedman, Law and Policy Project, Columbia University School of Public Health; Holly Burkhalter, Advocacy Director of PHR; Holly Atkinson, M.D., President and C.E.O., Reuters Health Information Services; and Michele Heisler, M.D., M.P.A., Department of Internal Medicine, University of Michigan.

Heidi Bauer, M.D., M.P.H., Alameda County Medical Center, Department of Internal Medicine, Oakland, CA; and Michele Manos, Ph.D, University of California San Francisco, Department of Epidemiology and Biostatistics, San Francisco, CA., contributed to data analysis and writing related to PHR's health and human rights survey. Drs. Bauer and Manos are volunteer consultants to Physicians for Human Rights. The report is based on research undertaken by PHR during a three-month period in early 1998. The report was reviewed and edited by Leonard Rubenstein, J.D., Susannah Sirkin, M.Ed., and Barbara Ayotte, all of Physicians for Human Rights.

This research was supported by a grant from the Edna McConnell Clark Foundation, New York, NY. The authors are grateful to the organizations that facilitated access to, and collection of, information used in this study. We are especially grateful to the Afghan women who participated in this study despite years of suffering.

GLOSSARY

Burqa: A head to toe covering for women that has only a mesh cloth to see and breathe through.

Chador: A veil that is culturally specific and variable among different Islamic countries.

Hijab: Modest clothing (for women or men) that is culturally specific and variable among different Islamic countries.

ICRC: International Committee of the Red Cross.

Jihad: A holy war.

Madrasas: Religious (Islamic) schools in Pakistan.

Mahram: A family member who is a husband, father, brother, or son.

Mujaheddin: Freedom fighters

MSF: Médecins sans Frontières.

Qur'an: The sacred book of Islam.

Pashto: The language of the Pashtun ethnic group.

Pashtun: An ethnic group of Afghanistan.

NGO: Non-governmental organization.

PHR: Physicians for Human Rights.

Shura: A council.

UN: United Nations.

UNHCR: United Nations High Commissioner for Refugees.

UNICEF: United Nations Children's Fund.

UNOCHA: United Nations Office for the Coordination of Humanitarian Assistance in Afghanistan.

Wakeel: A community representative. *Wakeels* who represent city wards in Afghanistan are responsible for enlisting the needs of families in each

FOREWORD

For a Credible Islamic Affirmation of the Universality of Human Rights

As a Muslim man from Sudan, I vehemently condemn the gross and systematic persecution of women and other violations of international human rights law in Afghanistan documented by Physicians for Human Rights in this report. I also affirm my unqualified endorsement of the essential premise of the vitally important work of this and other human organizations around the world: that international human rights standards are universally valid and applicable as the legal entitlement of every human being, without discrimination on such grounds as gender or religion.

However, what is happening in Afghanistan today clearly shows that it is not enough for Muslims like myself to simply associate ourselves with the principled and highly professional efforts of organizations like Physicians for Human Rights. In addition to being proactive in making our contributions to such efforts, Muslims everywhere must equally vehemently challenge and rebut any alleged Islamic justification for any violations of human rights and humanitarian law. Muslims and their governments must strongly condemn human rights violations wherever they occur and whoever commits them, and not only when speaking out is convenient or politically expedient. This is particularly important, in my view, when violations are committed in the name of some alleged Islamic agenda. Otherwise, how can Muslims legitimately protest against negative stereotypes of Islam in the media as sanctioning terrorism, cruelty and inhumanity?

Debates about Islam and human rights continue in many Islamic societies around the world today, but that has nothing to do with what is happening in Afghanistan today. As even the most conservative or radical Muslims around the world know, most of the policies and practices of the Taliban government documented in this report have no Islamic justification whatsoever. Human rights organizations like Physicians for Human Rights are condemning these policies and practices from a human rights point of view. Unless Muslims do the same from an Islamic point of view as well, the Taliban will get away with their false claim that these heinous crimes against humanity are dictated by Islam as a religion.

— **Abdullahi A. An-Na'im, Ph.D.**
Professor of Law, Emory University
Formerly of the University of Khartoum, Sudan

I. EXECUTIVE SUMMARY

This report documents the results of a three-month study of women's health and human rights concerns and conditions in Afghanistan by Physicians for Human Rights (PHR). The extent to which the Taliban regime has threatened the human rights of Afghan women is unparalleled in recent history. Taliban policies of systematic discrimination against women seriously undermine the health and well-being of Afghan women. Such discrimination and the suffering it causes constitute an affront to the dignity and worth of Afghan women, and humanity as a whole.

The people of Afghanistan have suffered extensive human rights violations in the course of the past twenty years. The Soviet invasion and occupation from 1979 to 1989, aided by Afghan communist military and civilian collaborators, brought mass killings, torture, disappearance, the largest recorded refugee outflow in history, and a scourge of landmines. The subsequent civil war, fueled by support from neighboring countries and other regional powers for various factions following the collapse of the Soviet-backed regime in 1992, witnessed extensive abuses by the armed factions vying for power, including the virtual destruction of the capital city, Kabul, from rocket shelling, aerial bombardment and mortaring. Indiscriminate use of force, torture, killing in detention of both civilians and combatants, the extensive laying of antipersonnel landmines, and the arbitrary exercise of authority principally through military force characterized Afghanistan for much of this period.

In November 1994, a new group named "Taliban" emerged as a military and political force. Taliban, which means "students of Muslim religious studies," are poorly educated rural Pashtun youths mostly recruited from refugee camps and religious schools ("*madrasas*") in neighboring Pakistan. This movement, led by Mullah Mohammed Omar, a 31-year-old religious leader, claims to be restoring peace and security through the imposition of a strict Islamic order. With no functioning judicial system, many municipal and provincial authorities use the Taliban's interpretation of *Shari'a* (Islamic law) and traditional tribal codes of justice.[1]

---

[1] U.N. Department of Humanitarian Affairs (DHA), *Report of the DHA Mission to Afghanistan*, [Hereafter *DHA Report*] 15 June 1997, at 1.1

The Taliban is the first faction laying claim to power in Afghanistan that has targeted women for extreme repression and punished them brutally for infractions. To PHR's knowledge, no other regime in the world has methodically and violently forced half of its population into virtual house arrest, prohibiting them on pain of physical punishment from showing their faces, seeking medical care without a male escort, or attending school.

After taking control of the capital city of Kabul on September 26, 1996, the Taliban issued edicts[2] forbidding women to work outside the home, attend school, or to leave their homes unless accompanied by a husband, father, brother, or son. In public, women must be covered from head to toe in a *burqa*, a body-length covering with only a mesh opening to see and breathe through. Women are not permitted to wear white (the color of the Taliban flag) socks or white shoes, or shoes that make noise while they are walking. Also, houses and buildings in public view must have their windows painted over if females are present in these places.

Furthermore, in January 1997, Taliban officials announced a policy of segregating men and women into separate hospitals.[3] This regulation was not strictly enforced until September 1997 when the Ministry of Public Health ordered all hospitals in Kabul to suspend medical services to the city's half million women at all but one, poorly-equipped hospital for women.[4] Female medical workers also were banned from working in Kabul's 22 hospitals. The temporary Rabia Balkhi facility was designated the sole facility available to women. At that time the facility had 35 beds and no clean water, electricity, surgical equipment, X-ray machines, suction, or oxygen.[5] An international uproar ensued, and in November 1997, after two months of negotiations with the International Committee of the Red Cross, the Taliban partially rescinded its directive and agreed to reopen some of the hospitals and make available limited beds therein. Despite the reversal, however, Taliban gender restrictions— preventing women from moving freely and prohibiting women from working— continue to interfere with the delivery of health services and humanitarian assistance to women and girls.[6]

---

[2] See Appendices A,B, and C.

[3] *U.S. Department of State Country Report on Human Rights Practices.* Washington, DC: U.S. Department of State; 1998 [Hereafter *Country Report on Human Rights.*].

[4] Block, M. Kabul's health apartheid. *The Nation.* November 24, 1997:5-6.

[5] Consequences of the new public health policy decisions regarding female health care in Kabul, Afghanistan, A briefing paper by Médecins sans Frontières, September 1997.

[6] *Country Report on Human Rights, Supra,* 3

The Taliban's edicts restricting women's rights have had a disastrous impact on Afghan women and girls' access to education, as well as health care. One of the first edicts issued by the regime when it rose to power was to prohibit girls and women from attending school. Humanitarian groups initiated projects to replace through philanthropy what prior governments had afforded as a right to both sexes.[7] Hundreds of girl's schools were established in private homes and thousands of women and girls were taught to sew and weave.

On June 16, 1998, the Taliban ordered the closing of more than 100 privately funded schools where thousands of young women and girls were receiving training in skills that would have helped them support their families. The Taliban issued new rules for nongovernmental organizations providing the schooling: education must be limited to girls up to the age of eight, and restricted to the *Qur'an*.[8]

Taliban policies that restrict women's rights and deny basic needs are often brutally and arbitrary enforced by the "religious police" (Department for the Propagation of Virtue and the Suppression of Vice) usually in the form of summary, public beatings.[9] In addition, Afghan staff members of international organizations have reportedly faced threats, harassment, beating and arrest in the course of conducting their professional duties.[10]

PHR's researcher when visiting Kabul in 1998, saw a city of beggars — women who had once been teachers and nurses now moving in the streets like ghosts under their enveloping *burqas*, selling every possession and begging so as to feed their children. It is difficult to find another government or would-be government in the world that has deliberately created such poverty by arbitrarily depriving half the population under its control of jobs, schooling, mobility, and health care. Such restrictions are literally life threatening to women and to their children.

The Taliban's abuses are by no means limited to women. Thousands of men have been taken prisoner, arbitrarily detained, tortured, and many killed and disappeared. Men are beaten and jailed for wearing beards of insufficient length (that of a clenched fist beneath the chin),

---

[7] Historically, Afghan women suffered over 80% illiteracy, but it was not based on legal prohibitions on their attendance in school. Afghanistan had free public education for all before the Taliban, but facilities for schooling of both boys and girls were poor and scarce in rural areas. And conservative families often restricted girls' access to public education.

[8] 100 Girls' Schools in Afghan Capital Are Ordered Shut, *The New York Times*, June 17, 1998. (Associated Press, June 16, 1998.)

[9] *Country Report on Human Rights, Supra*, 3.

[10] *Id.*

are subjected to cruel and degrading conditions in jail, and suffer such punishments as amputation and stoning. Men are also vulnerable to extortion, arrest, gang rape,[11] and abuse in detention because of their ethnicity or presumed political views.[12] The Taliban's *Shari'a* courts lack even a semblance of due process, with no provisions for legal counsel and frequent use of torture to extract confessions.[13]

Afghanistan's history of civil war and particularly the period of anarchy between 1992 and 1995 following the collapse of the Communist regime has contributed to the perception outside Afghanistan that while the Taliban is repressive, at least it has stopped the war and ended violent crime in the capital.[14]

Physicians for Human Rights rejects this assessment of Afghanistan under the Taliban. For nearly twenty years, the Afghan people have suffered the health consequences of armed conflict and human rights violations. That Taliban officials now claim to be "restoring peace"[15] to Afghanistan is perhaps one of the cruelest ironies of our time, as they have virtually imprisoned Afghan women in their homes and threatened

---

[11] Physicians for Human Rights obtained first-hand information about two cases of gang rape of boys by Taliban police. One was thirteen, the other eighteen years old. The thirteen-year-old child had been abducted following a fight with the son of a Taliban supporter. In prison, he reported being beaten and raped. The eighteen-year-old reported that he had been held for eight days during which time he was repeatedly raped; as a consequence, his health has been severely compromised. Both of the boys are Hazara, who are particularly vulnerable to Taliban depredations.

[12] Shiite men or men of Hazara, Tajik, or Uzbek ethnicity are presumed to support the opposition Northern Alliance.

[13] In April 1998, Amnesty International reported: In recent months, at least five men convicted of sodomy [presumed to be homosexuals] by Taliban *Shari'a* courts have been placed next to standing walls by Taliban officials and then buried under the rubble as the walls were toppled upon them. At least four alleged murderers have been executed in public by the family members of the murdered persons. At least five men have had their hands amputated on allegation of theft, and at least one man and one woman have been flogged by Taliban officials on allegation of adultery. *Afghanistan: Flagrant abuse of the right to life and dignity*, Amnesty International, April 1998.

[14] A sample of this view might be seen in a letter to the British medical journal, *The Lancet* on June 28, 1997. Four writers based in Pakistan and affiliated with "HealthNet International," write "Afghanistan has been at war for almost 20 years. About 40% of Kabul is mine-infested rubble, and... the infrastructure of the country has broken down. Theft, looting, rape, and torture were commonplace for the 3 years before the arrival of the Taliban in Kabul, and it was only possible to travel between cities in armed convoys. Currently, theft is rare, the Taliban do not rape women and severely punish anyone who does, and it is possible to travel in all areas, apart from where there is fighting."

[15] *DHA Report*, *Supra*,1 at 1.1.

their very survival. The "peace" imposed on that portion of the country under Taliban rule is the peace of the *burqa*, the quiet of women and girls cowering in their homes, and the silence of a citizenry terrorized by the Taliban's violent and arbitrary application of their version of *Shari'a* law.

Methods of Investigation

Although Taliban restrictions on women have been highly publicized,[16] very little is known about the experiences and opinions of Afghan women. This study was designed to assess the health and human rights concerns and conditions of a broad spectrum of Afghan women[17] who have lived in Kabul under Taliban rule and whose concerns otherwise may not have been represented. Marked restriction on the movement of women, prohibition on interactions with expatriates, and the risk of summary punishment for acts which authorities consider threatening present considerable challenges to an effective study design. PHR's strategy for documenting the health and human rights problems of Afghan women included both qualitative and quantitative methods in researching three different sources of evidence (methodological triangulation). This approach facilitated corroboration between different sources of evidence and methods.

The three components of the study included: 1) a women's health and human rights survey of 160 Afghan women, 2) forty case testimonies of Afghan women, and 3) interviews with 12 humanitarian assistance providers, health personnel or other experts. In addition, the direct observations of PHR's investigator have enhanced the documentation. The domains of inquiry for each study component included Afghan women's: 1) physical health status and access to health care, 2) mental health status, 3) war-related trauma and landmine exposures, 4) experiences of abuse by Taliban officials, and 5) attitudes toward women's human rights.

The information included in this report was collected during a three-month period in the beginning of 1998. Women who participated in the health and human rights survey and case testimonies were from all walks of life, ethnic groups, educational levels and economic backgrounds. The participants included women currently living in Kabul and

---

[16] See Crossette B. Afghan women demanding end to their repression by militants. *New York Times*. April 6, 1998:A1; Erlanger S. Albright, in Pakistan, Hammers Taliban. *New York Times*; November 18, 1997: A1; and Taliban's war on women. *New York Times*. November 15, 1997.

[17] The results of this study may not be generalizable to all women in Afghanistan. Considering the current conditions of repression of women in Afghanistan, the sampling strategy used in the study aimed to assess the health and human rights experiences and attitudes of the most diverse group of Afghan women possible.

Afghan women who recently migrated to Pakistan. All participants lived in Kabul for most of their lives and for at least one year after the Taliban took control of Kabul in September 1996.

Participants for the health and human rights survey included women who were randomly selected from lists of humanitarian assistance providers and chain (or snowball)[18] samples of women with initial cases being referred by humanitarian assistance providers. Women interviewed for case testimonies were selected using chain sampling, again with initial cases referred by humanitarian assistance providers. In all cases the findings contained in this report are based on PHR's independent selection of case material and analysis of data, testimony, and other documentation.

Summary of Findings

The results of the survey of 160 Afghan women indicated that the extension of the Taliban's authority in Afghanistan has had debilitating consequences for women's health and human rights there. 71% of participants reported a decline in their physical health over the past two years. The majority of respondents (77%) reported poor access to health care services in Kabul over the past year of residence there; an additional 20% reported no access. Both the access to care and the quality of health care services in Kabul were deemed "much worse" over the past year compared with two years prior by a majority of the participants (62% and 58%, respectively). In addition, fifty-three percent of women described occasions in which they were seriously ill and unable to seek medical care. 28% of the Afghan women reported inadequate control over their own reproduction.

The women interviewed by PHR consistently described high levels of poor health, multiple specific symptoms, and a significant decline in women's physical condition since the beginning of the Taliban occupation. Sixty-six percent of women interviewed described a decline in their physical condition over the past two years. An Afghan physician described declining nutrition in children, an increasing rate of tuberculosis, and a high prevalence of other infectious diseases among women and children.

PHR visited the Rabia Balkhi Hospital, previously the only facility in Kabul open to women, and found that it lacked basic medical supplies and equipment such as X-ray machines, suction and oxygen, running water, and medications. Women housed there said they had received no medical attention; one had not been attended to for ten days.

---

[18] Chain sampling consisted of identifying initial participants through humanitarian assistance organizations, then identifying additional cases from the participants, and so on. See Patton MQ. *Qualitative Evaluation and Research Methods.* Newbury Park, CA: Sage Publications; 1990:169-283.

At the only maternity hospital in Kabul, Maiwand, there were seven or eight beds to a room and, in one room, two patients shared one bed. One woman was losing her child because of RH incompatibility and no available antigen. Some of the women interviewed by PHR were experiencing abnormal bleeding during pregnancy. Some were given a prescription but they had not bought it because they couldn't afford it; other women had been at the hospital for days and had received no treatment at all.

Yet even these poor facilities are not available to many women who seek treatment for themselves or their children. In the semi-structured interviews with 40 Afghan women, PHR explored the reasons for decreased access to health care services. Of the 40 women interviewed, 87% (33 of 38) reported a decrease in their access to health services. The reasons given included: no chaperone available (27%), restrictions on women's mobility (36%), hospital refused to provide care (21%), no female doctor available (48%), do not own a burqa (6%), and economics (61%).

Male doctors' access to sick children within women's hospitals is also severely curtailed, leading to unnecessary death. A female physician reported that a female child died of the measles because the authorities didn't allow a male doctor to visit the children's ward, which is located within a designated female ward of a local hospital.[19]

A twenty-year-old woman interviewed in Kabul related the following:

> *"Eight months ago, my two-and-a-half year old daughter died from diarrhea. She was refused treatment by the first hospital that we took her to. The second hospital mistreated her [they refused to provide intravenous fluids and antibiotics because of their Hazara ethnicity, according to the respondent]. Her body was handed to me and her father in the middle of the night. With her body in my arms, we left the hospital. It was curfew time and we had a long way to get home. We had to spend the night inside a destroyed house among the rubble. In the morning we took my dead baby home but we had no money for her funeral."[20]*

Another woman had a similar experience:

> *"Women are not admitted in several hospitals. My niece had severe diarrhea. We took her to Aliabad hospital, but they refused to see her. They asked us to take her to a private doctor, but we couldn't afford a private doctor's fee. She barely survived."[21]*

---

[19] PHR Interview, K15, Kabul, Afghanistan.

[20] PHR Interview, K6, Kabul, Afghanistan.

[21] PHR Interview, K4, Kabul, Afghanistan.

The requirement, reiterated in June 1998, that physicians may not treat women unaccompanied by close male relatives, has caused particular problems for the many women in Kabul and elsewhere who do not have male relatives to play this role. In Kabul alone, there are more than 30,000 widows.[22] As one survey respondent stated: "I can't see a male doctor since I don't have a chaperone to accompany me; my brother is too young and my father is ill. I have no other male chaperone to accompany me to the doctor's office."[23]

The Taliban's interference in the provision of health care is not limited to segregation of the hospitals. Taliban guards are ever present in medical facilities and intervene at will on behalf of the Department for the Propagation of Virtue and the Suppression of Vice. Nurses and other female health personnel may be beaten when not covered completely, and women often fear to even venture from their homes to seek health care for themselves or their children.[24]

Male physicians cannot properly examine women patients because of prohibitions on touching them or looking at their bodies. A dentist said he only examined a woman's teeth if a lookout was posted at the door while he lifted her veil. He noted that if he were caught treating a woman, he and his patient would be beaten, and the authorities would likely close his office and throw him in jail.

Women's fear of being publicly beaten or arrested by the Taliban for being on the street discourages many of them from even attempting to seek health care. PHR interviewed homeless, displaced women occupying an abandoned school with their children. One woman was mourning the recent death of her 20-year-old daughter, who had suffered from stomach pains for days but could not be taken out because her mother did not possess a *burqa*. The women gathered there begged the PHR researcher to send them some *burqas* from the United States so that they could go out on the street. They didn't possess the garment, and had no money to pay for it.[25]

The wearing of the *burqa* itself may contribute to health problems. In answer to a question in the PHR survey, a female pediatrician noted the

---

[22] E/CN. 4/1997/59 Final report on the situation of human rights in Afghanistan submitted by Mr. Choong-Hyun Paik, Special Rapporteur, in accordance with Commission on Human Rights resolution 1996/75). [Hereafter, *E/CN.4/1997/59*].

[23] Interview, K1, Kabul, Afghanistan.

[24] Health Care Under the Taliban, *The Lancet*, Vol. 349, April 26, 1997.

[25] Before the Taliban, few urban dwellers owned a *burqa*, as it was not typically worn in Afghanistan. In Kabul, a very cheap *burqa* costs approximately $9.00 US, which is much more than most Afghan women can now afford.

following: "My activities are restricted. Walking with the *burqa* is difficult; it has so many health hazards. You can't see well and there is a risk of falling or getting hit by a car. Also, for women with asthma or hypertension, wearing a *burqa* is very unhealthy."[26] A doctor informed PHR that the garment may cause eye problems and poor vision, poor hearing, skin rash, headaches, increased cardiac problems and asthma, itching of the scalp, alopecia (hair loss), and depression. Another respondent noted that the "*burqa* is another reason for not wanting to go outside the house. I am not used to wearing the *burqa* and it is a risk for me every time I wear it. I can fall and break my leg or my neck, also, it is not good for the eyes."[27]

Participants in the health and human rights survey also reported extraordinarily high levels of mental stress and depression. 81% of participants reported a decline in their mental condition. A large percentage of respondents (42%)[28] met the diagnostic criteria for post-traumatic stress disorder (PTSD) (based on the *Diagnostical and Statistical Manual of Mental Disorders, Fourth Edition*) and major depression (97%), and also demonstrated significant symptoms of anxiety (86%) Twenty-one percent of the participants indicated that they had suicidal thoughts "extremely often" or "quite often". It is clear from PHR's forty interviews with Afghan women that the general climate of cruelty, abuse, and tyranny that characterizes Taliban rule has had a profound affect on women's mental health. Ninety-five percent of women interviewed described a decline in their mental condition over the past two years.

The denial of education also contributes to Afghan women's deteriorating mental health. All of the women interviewed by PHR indicated that they had become unemployed due to Taliban policies, and 74% indicated that they are now unemployed as well. The interviews revealed that women attributed the anxiety and depression that affects the vast majority of them to their fear of limited opportunities for their children, specifically denial of education to girl children. Poor and uneducated women spoke with particular urgency of their desire to obtain education for children, and saw health care, schooling, and protection of human rights as a key towards achieving a better future.

Humanitarian assistance providers have played a critical role in meeting the basic needs of the Afghan people. However, in striking contrast

---

[26] PHR Interview, K20, Kabul, Afghanistan.

[27] PHR Interview, K19, Kabul, Afghanistan.

[28] Even higher percentages reported significant intrusive (94%) and arousal (95%) symptoms of PTSD.

to published reports indicating the successful disbursement of humanitarian assistance,[29] only 6% of respondents reported receiving any form of humanitarian assistance while living in Kabul. In addition to reported corruption in the distribution of aid, Taliban gender restrictions inevitably interfere with the delivery of humanitarian assistance to women.[30] A Taliban decree dated July 20, 1997, for example, stated that women could not pick up food or other aid from distribution centers themselves. A male relative had to pick up and deliver the aid to the women. Widows are particularly vulnerable to exclusion by such requirements.

The Taliban's claim that its policy of gender segregation is rooted in Afghan history and culture is invalidated by the experience and views of Afghan women themselves. Afghan women have a long history of participation in Afghan society and in political and economic life, including employment as health professionals, teachers, and in government offices. PHR's interviews with 160 women represented a diverse sample of Afghan women living or having recently lived in Kabul under Taliban rule. Virtually all study participants agreed that women should have equal access to education, equal work opportunities, freedom of expression, freedom of association, freedom of movement, control over the number and spacing of children, legal protection for women's human rights, and participation in government. Over 95 percent disagreed with Taliban dress codes and the proposition that the teaching of Islam imposes restrictions on women's human rights.

The Afghan women in PHR's health and human rights survey also reported a high prevalence of loss of a family member to war and displacement hardships. Eighty-four percent of women reported one or more family members killed in war.[31] All but one of the participants had been displaced from Kabul at least once. More than 80% of all respondents were displaced one or more times within Kabul between 1992 and September 1996. The most commonly cited hardships during displacement included poverty (69%), disease (68%), emotional difficulties (63%), lack of access to health care services (54%), lack of access to education (51%), and inadequate sanitation (50%).

---

[29] Report of the Special Rapporteur on the situation of human rights in Afghanistan: Question of the violation of human rights and fundamental freedoms in any part of the world, with particular reference to colonial and other dependent countries and territories. Geneva, Switzerland: United Nations Commission on Human Rights; United Nations document E/CN.4/1996/64. [Hereafter, *E/CN. 4/1996/64*]

[30] *Country Report on Human Rights, Supra*, 3.

[31] Seventy percent reported war-related injuries among their family members.

Many of those surveyed reported injury and death within their family from landmines.[32] Sixteen percent of those surveyed reported that landmines killed one or more family members, and 23% reported injuries to family members caused by landmines. In spite of the high rates of injury and death, only 48% of respondents had received landmine awareness education or training. Among 113 women with children, 62% reported that their children had received landmine awareness education or training.

PHR's health and human rights survey demonstrates that harassment and physical abuse of Afghan women and their family members by Taliban officials is extremely common in Kabul. Sixty-nine percent of women reported that they or a family member had been detained in Kabul by Taliban religious police or security forces. Twenty-two percent of women reported a total of 43 separate incidents in which they were detained and abused. Of these incidents, 72% followed non-adherence to the Taliban's dress code for women.[33] The majority (35/43, 81%) of detentions lasted less than one hour; however, 36 (84%) resulted in public beatings and one (2%) in torture.[34]

Over half (58%) of the study participants reported that a family member had been detained in a total of 133 separate incidents. Of the 17 incidents involving female family members, the reasons for detention and

---

[32] It is estimated that since 1992, landmines have killed more than 20,000 people and injured more than 400,000 others in Afghanistan. Approximately 80% of the landmine casualties are civilian and among these, 40-50% are women and children. See *Country Report on Human Rights, Supra,* 3

[33] Specific offenses included: not wearing a *burqa*; not completely covering the face, hands, wrists or feet; wearing stylish clothes, white socks or white shoes, or shoes that make noise when walking. Five (12%) respondents were detained for being unaccompanied by a male chaperone in public. Among other detainees, two disabled women (leg amputees from rocket blast injuries) were detained and beaten for entering through a designated male entrance in a public building.

[34] In this report, the term "torture" is defined according to the United Nations Convention Against Torture; that is, "any act by which severe pain or suffering, whether physical or mental, is intentionally inflicted on a person for such purposes as obtaining from him or a third person information or a confession, punishing him for an act he or a third person has committed or is suspected of having committed, or intimidating or coercing him or a third person for any reason based on discrimination of any kind, when such pain or suffering is inflicted by or at the instigation of or with the consent or acquiescence of a public official or other person acting in an official capacity" in *Twenty-Five Human Rights Documents* (New York: Center for the Study of Human Rights, Columbia University, 1994), p. 148. Torture is considered to be "systematic" in this report when: "it is apparent that the torture cases reported have not occurred fortuitously in a particular place or at a particular time, but are seen to be habitual, widespread and deliberate in at least a considerable part of the territory of the country...". See the definition by The Committee Against Torture (CAT), UN Document A/48/44/Add.1, para. 58.

abuse were similar to those identified by the respondents. Of the 116 incidents involving male family members, reasons for detention included having a short beard (29, 25%)[35] and being a member of a minority ethnic group (mainly Tajik and Hazara) (32, 28%).[36] Fifty-four percent of these detentions resulted in beatings and 21% resulted in torture. Under these circumstances, 68% of women surveyed reported that they had "extremely restricted" their activities in public during the past year in Kabul.

PHR's interviews with 40 Afghan women corroborated experiences of detention and abuse of Afghan women and their families by Taliban officials. Sixty-eight percent of women interviewed described incidents in which they were detained and physically abused by Taliban officials. The reasons for abuse and types of abuse experienced paralleled that reported in PHR's health and human rights survey.

The atmosphere of fear created by the Taliban laws and their harsh imposition has exacerbated the multiple traumas related by the women PHR interviewed. PHR gained firsthand knowledge of those experiences while in Kabul.[37] Every Friday, the Taliban terrorizes the city of Kabul by publicly punishing alleged wrongdoers in the Kabul sports stadium and requiring public attendance at the floggings, shootings, hangings, beheadings, and amputations.[38]

On one occasion, PHR's researcher, herself, witnessed the public execution (stabbing and beheading) of two men convicted of murder by the Taliban *Shari'a* court at the sports stadium, and another day saw the amputation of an alleged thief's hand and the flogging of an eighteen-year-old girl who was accused of having a romantic relationship. Witnesses told PHR that another young woman died a few days after being subjected to a public flogging for a similar charge. Reportedly, she either committed suicide or was killed by her father because of the embarrassment and shame of the punishment. The researcher said that before,

---

[35] According to Taliban edicts, men's beards must protrude farther than would a fist clamped at the base of the chin; men who do not comply are subjected to public beatings, torture, and imprisonment. See *Country Report on Human Rights, Supra*,3.

[36] Another 47% were detained for a variety of reasons, including not being in a mosque at prayer time, flying a kite, playing music at their wedding, and laughing in public.

[37] The organization's researcher herself narrowly escaped a beating when she was pursued by a young member of the security forces brandishing a whip, as he screamed at her for exposing her wrists and for being alone in public.

[38] Amnesty International reported on March 13, 1998, that over 30,000 spectators (made up of women and boys) were summoned by loudspeaker to gather at Kabul's sports stadium to watch the father and brother of a murdered man shoot an alleged murderer who had been sentenced to death by a Taliban *Shari'a* court. *Afghanistan: Flagrant abuse of the right to life and dignity, Supra*, 13.

during, and after the execution and punishments, the stadium was filled with women and children crying and pleading with the authorities not to carry out the sentences, albeit in vain.[39]

Witnessing executions, fleeing religious police with whips who search for women and girls diverging from dress codes or other edicts, having a family member jailed or beaten; such experiences traumatize and retraumatize Afghan women, who have already experienced the horrors of war, rocketing, ever-present landmines and unexploded ordnance, and the loss of friends and immediate family.[40]

Recommendations

In recent years, Physicians for Human Rights and many leaders in public health have argued that health, defined as "a state of complete physical, mental and social well-being and not merely the absence of disease or infirmity,"[41] requires the protection and promotion of human rights.[42] In Afghanistan, Taliban restrictions on Afghan women's freedom of expression, association, and movement deny women full participation in society, and consequently, from effectively securing equal opportunities for work, education, and access to health. Furthermore, such exclusion of women from employment and education jeopardizes their capacity to survive and participate in society. The health and human rights concerns of Afghan women identified in this study illustrate that the promotion of Afghan women's health is inseparable from the protection and promotion of human rights.

---

[39] The researcher saw a number of women who were apparently family members on the field at the execution site. The executions were carried out in front of them; following the beheadings, the women, shrouded in *burqa*, continued crouching next to the bodies.

[40] Such sights and experiences also traumatize children. During an interview at the home of a woman several days after a public beheading, a young boy in the home was continually crying. When the researcher asked why he was crying, the child, who had actually been forced to witness the execution, said that he was frightened because of the killings going on around him.

[41] World Health Organization. *Declaration of Alma Ata*. World Health Organization, Primary Health Care. WHO Geneva. 1978.

[42] See Iacopino V. Human Rights: Health Concerns for the Twenty-First Century. In: Majumdar SK, Rosenfeld LM, Nash DB, Audet AM, eds. *Medicine and Health Care into the Twenty-First Century*. Philadelphia: Pennsylvania Academy of Science. 1995:376-392; Mann J. Health and Human Rights. *Health and Human Rights*. 1994; 1(1):6-23; The Consortium for Health and Human Rights, Health and Human Rights, A Call to Action: The 50th Anniversary of the Universal Declaration of Human Rights. *JAMA*. 1998; 280(5):462-464; and Ely-Yamin, A. Transformative combinations: women's health and human rights. *JAMWA*; 52(4):169-173.

Afghanistan has been the focus of extensive efforts by the United Nations for two decades. A Special Rapporteur to monitor human rights is in place and has issued many detailed reports. A Special Envoy to the Secretary General visits regularly, and a Special Mission for Afghanistan has been established. The General Assembly has passed numerous resolutions calling upon all parties to cease their violations of human rights, and UN interlocutors have been attempting to mediate the conflict for the past six years. Hundreds of millions of dollars worth of humanitarian aid have been spent both within Afghanistan and in Pakistan to support Afghan refugees. Yet Afghanistan today is a monument to the avarice of the warring parties that brought it to this point, to the international and Afghan actors who promoted the Taliban, and to the United Nations' failure.[43]

PHR urges the international community to reconsider the situation of Afghanistan and take action aimed at securing a representative government, which is committed to international human rights standards, including the equal rights for women. In particular, those governments, that support the Taliban, notably Pakistan, should be publicly called upon to end their support for the regime, and an effective arms embargo should be established. International human rights monitors should be deployed to collect and publicly disseminate information on rights abuses by all parties from all parts of the country.

The UN's Memorandum of Understanding with the Taliban, which acknowledges that access for women to health care and education in Afghanistan must be "gradual", should be rescinded and renegotiated.

If the UN fails to reach an agreement that would assure the immediate access of Afghan women and girls to health care and education and an end to restrictions on the operations of humanitarian organizations (including limits on the movement of their Muslim female staff) then it should publicly announce that it is terminating negotiations with the Taliban, restricting its aid to humanitarian operations carried out by nongovernmental organizations, and removing UN staff from Afghanistan to the maximum extent feasible.

---

[43] In *Fundamentalism Reborn? Afghanistan and the Taliban*(Vanguard Books, Lahore Pakistan, Pakistan, 1998) author William Maley cites the U.N. itself on the failure of its mission in Afghanistan: "...it could be argued that ... the role of the United Nations in Afghanistan is little more than that of an alibi to provide cover for the inaction — or worse — of the international community at large." The Situation in Afghanistan and its Implications for International Peace and Security: Report of the Secretary General, 14 November 1997.

Summary of Specific Recommendations:

To the Taliban:

- The Taliban must commit themselves to take all measures necessary to stop the practice of systematic discrimination against women and guarantee women's human rights.
- Taliban officials must respect rights to due process as required by international human rights instruments under which it has assumed obligations. Those who breach rights to due process should be held criminally responsible and prosecuted in accordance with international human rights standards.
- All law enforcement and security personnel should be ordered to respect human rights and should receive adequate training in human rights standards, including women's human rights, prevention of violations, and prisoners' rights.
- Security personnel and others responsible for these abuses should be held criminally responsible and prosecuted in accordance with international human rights standards. Victims of abuse should receive fair and adequate compensation, including the means for as full rehabilitation as possible.

To the International Community:

- The international community must not accept any justifications for systematic discrimination against Afghan women. Representation of Afghanistan at the United Nations should not be afforded to any party whose policies, either explicit or implicit, discriminate against women.
- The international community should also consider ways in which those responsible for the vast degradation of women and girls in Afghanistan might be held accountable before the world for these human rights violations. The United Nations Human Rights Commission should call a special session for purposes of creating a Commission of Experts to investigate the systematic and egregious human rights violations against women in Afghanistan and to create measures to hold those responsible accountable.
- International human rights monitors should be deployed to collect and publicly disseminate information on rights abuses, especially those against women, by all parties and from all parts of the country.
- The UN's Memorandum of Understanding with the Taliban should be rescinded and re-negotiated. If the UN fails to reach an agreement that would assure the immediate access of Afghan women and girls to health care and education and an end to restrictions on the operations of humanitarian organizations (including limits on the movement of their Muslim female staff), then it should publicly announce that it is terminating negotiations, restricting its aid to humanitarian operations

carried out by non-governmental organizations, and removing UN staff from Afghanistan to the maximum extent feasible.

To Health and Humanitarian Assistance Providers:
- Humanitarian intervention programs should reevaluate aid distribution procedures to ensure that those most in need are not discriminated against. One way to accomplish this would be for agencies to develop impact assessments regarding human rights, especially women's human rights, which they should factor into their policy decisions and field procedures. In particular, the system of distributing assistance through local political leaders (*wakeels*) should be reviewed, as there is evidence to suggest that these individuals, in many cases, are not distributing the assistance to those most in need.
- Providers of humanitarian assistance in Afghanistan have been all but shut down by the Taliban, which has increasingly interfered with their operations, by closing down private schools for girls, prohibiting women from directly receiving humanitarian aid, and by ordering relief workers out of the city and into inhabitable barracks on Kabul's outskirts. As a consequence, almost all relief providers left Kabul in late July. This vacuum will almost certainly result in enormous added privation, especially for women and girls. PHR urges those providers who remain in Afghanistan to protest restrictions and discrimination and redouble their efforts to overcome these in their administration of humanitarian assistance.
- At such time as humanitarian aid workers are permitted to resume operations in Afghanistan, PHR urges them to reevaluate aid distribution procedures to assure that women and children receive the bulk of food aid. To the maximum extent feasible, health and humanitarian assistance providers must insist that distribution of aid and access to programs be carried out in a non-discriminatory manner. They must make every effort to overcome the barriers to women's receipt of assistance.
- The extent of mental health problems identified in this study indicates an urgent need for humanitarian organizations to provide mental health services for women.
- Afghan women who seek refuge outside of Afghanistan should be officially recognized as refugees by the United Nations High Commission for Refugees (UNHCR) and afforded assistance accordingly.
- Finally, international donors should continue their humanitarian assistance to refugees in Pakistan and Iran and ensure that their aid is distributed without discrimination. They should pay close attention to the needs of newly arriving refugees in Pakistan, who appear to be wholly underserved and are in need of shelter, food, and health services.

To Multinational Corporations:

- Corporate investment in Afghanistan directly and indirectly aids the Taliban regime, and contributes to the suffering of the Afghan people, especially women. For this reason, PHR calls for a moratorium on investment in Afghanistan, including the oil and gas pipelines proposed by a consortium of multinational corporations, including UNOCAL, based in California, and Bridas of Argentina.[44] Such a moratorium should remain in place until women are guaranteed their human rights.

To the United States Government:

- The United States should follow through on Secretary Albright's demand that the Taliban protect and promote the human rights of women in Afghanistan. The United States should take every opportunity to condemn the Taliban's oppression of women in international fora and to demand that the Taliban adhere to the requirements of international law.
- The United States should make plain that it does not and will not recognize any government that systematically disenfranchises women. It should oppose a claim by the Taliban for a seat at the United Nations as the government of Afghanistan.
- The United States should continue to maintain a leading role in peace negotiations between Taliban and anti-Taliban forces. These negotiations must include provisions to end the systematic discrimination of women in Afghanistan. "Peace" will come to Afghanistan only when women's human rights are protected and promoted in Afghanistan.
- The United States should call upon the government of Pakistan and other governments that support the Taliban to end that support.
- The United States should do all that is possible to include the protection and promotion of women's human rights in humanitarian assistance policies. It should denounce restrictions on humanitarian aid imposed by the Taliban and urge nations and NGOs providing aid to find ways of circumventing these restrictions.
- The United States should work with UN officials and other countries to designate Afghan women who flee gender-based persecution by the Taliban as refugees.

---

[44] See Chapter II.

II. INTRODUCTION

Background

Afghanistan, formerly known as the Republic of Afghanistan, was re-named as the Islamic State of Afghanistan in April 1992.[45] Situated at the crossroads of Central Asia, South Asia, West Asia and the Middle East, Afghanistan is a landlocked country mostly surrounded by rugged mountains and hills. The territory covers some 252,000 sq.mi (648,800 sq. km.), nearly identical in size to the State of Texas. It shares borders with the independent Central Asian States of Tajikistan, Uzbekistan and Turkmenistan, in the north; Xinjiang province of China, in the northeast; Iran in the west, and Pakistan in the east. The capital city, Kabul, is one of the largest cities in Afghanistan and had an estimated population of 1.5 million in 1996. Other major cities with a population of 50,000 to 200,000 people include Harat, Kandahar, Mazar-I-Sharif, Jalalabad, and Kundoz. Estimates of the total population of Afghanistan range between 15-20 million, including refugees in other countries.

More than 99.9% of Afghan people are Muslim, about 20% Shiite and 80% Sunni Muslims. Non-Muslim groups, including Hindus, Sikhs, and Jews make up less than 0.1% of the population. Although the vast majority of its people share a common religion, Afghanistan is very diverse in terms of language and ethnicity. Among several distinct ethnic groups living in Afghanistan are the Pashu-speaking Pashtuns (45-50%); Afghan-Persian or Dari-speaking Tajiks (25-30%); the Hazaragi (Persian dialect)-speaking Hazaras, (10-12%); and the Turkic-speaking Uzbeks, Turkomens, Kirghiz and Kazakh (10%). The two official languages are Persian and Pashto.[46] The climate in Afghanistan is dry with four seasons, including hot summers, cold winters, and heavy snow year-round in the mountainous regions.

Afghanistan has had a turbulent history. Before the mid-18th century it had been, at various times, a part of many different empires—Persian, Greek, Mongol, Mughal, Indian, Turkic, and others. With the formation

---

[45] Shahrani N, Afghanistan, in Simon R, Matter P and Bulleit R eds. *Encyclopedia of the Modern Middle East*. New York: Macmillan References USA, 1996. [Hereafter, *Encyclopedia of the Modern Middle East*]

[46] *Id*, at p.1

of the Pashtun tribal confederation in 1747, led by Ahamd Shah Durrani of the Durrani tribe, Afghanistan began to establish an independent identity. The convergence of ethnically distinct groups shaped Afghanistan's early political structure through a process of conciliation between competitive interests and the strengthening of a system of central governance under a Pashtun dynasty.[47] Since the mid-18th century, the Pashtun ethnic group has played a dominant role in Afghanistan's political history.

Throughout the 19th century, Afghanistan was a battleground for the rivalry between Britain and Russia in their attempts to control Central Asia. Twice, the British attempted to secure the northern border of British India by extending their rule into Afghanistan, first from 1838 to 1842 and then in 1879. On both occasions, the British troops had to withdraw, unable to maintain their military presence in Afghanistan. However, the second attempt allowed the British to retain some control over Afghan foreign affairs until the 1921 peace treaty of Rawalpindi recognized the full independence of Afghanistan.

King Amanullah (1919-1929), having gained Afghan independence in 1921,[48] launched a series of secular, liberal constitutional reforms similar to those developed by Mustafa Kemal Ataturk of Turkey, in an effort to modernize the country. The reforms opened Afghanistan to the outside world and introduced modern schools and education programs. He introduced Afghanistan's first Constitution in 1923 in an attempt to organize Afghan central authority on rational and predictable tenets. Women were allowed to unveil and initiatives were taken to promote their education. King Amanullah's reforms led to a rebellion-labeled as *jihad* (a "holy war") and which ended in his downfall.

In the 1930's, under King Zahir, renewed attempts to modernize Afghanistan were more modest and urban oriented.[49] Modern education was reintroduced in the cities and the foundation of Kabul University were laid down. In 1964, a new liberal Constitution was introduced under King Zahir with a system of elected parliamentary democracy. The next decade saw unprecedented liberalization in the political arena. Political parties emerged and a lively, relatively free political press came into being in Kabul. Contrary to the expectations of its proponents, the Afghan political structure became increasingly polarized under the liberalization process. Communism influenced students as fundamentalist Muslim ideology attracted a number of young intellectuals from the

---

[47] *DHA Report, Supra*, 1.

[48] *Id*, at 1.2.

[49] *Id*

rural areas and junior officers in the Afghan army. Among the nascent political parties were the communist People's Democratic Party of Afghanistan (PDPA), which would later rule the Democratic Republic of Afghanistan, and the Islamic Association (*Jamiat-i-islami*), from which a series of Islamic parties were formed during the resistance movement against the Soviet Union.[50]

In 1973 Mohammed Daoud, King Zahir's cousin and brother-in-law who served as Prime Minister under King Zahir, overthrew the constitutional monarchy and declared a republic. President Daoud suspended the free press and most of the political parties vanished with the exception of the PDPA. He limited relations with the Soviet Union and established contacts with Arab and Muslim countries. Meanwhile, his government initiated conciliatory discussions with Pakistan on the controversies that separated the two countries. Increasing distance of the Daoud regime from the Soviet Union led to further support of the PDPA opposition party and enabled it to take over the government in April 1978 in a bloody military coup, and to establish the Communist-led Democratic Republic of Afghanistan.

The end of the Pashtun dynasty and the take over by the Communists profoundly changed Afghan political life, to an extent that is still visible today. It marked a change from an aristocratic to a bureaucratic regime.[51] Noor Mohammed Taraki, the head of the PDPA was installed as President of the Revolutionary Council and Prime Minister. He renamed the country the Democratic Republic of Afghanistan (DRA), abolished the Constitution, and banned all opposition movements. Less than two months later, a coalition of two factions, the PDPA-Khalq (people) and the Parcham (Banner), fell apart.[52] Supported by the Soviet Union, Taraki attempted to create a Marxist state, but a nationwide rebellion, led by Islamic opposition groups and Muslim religious leaders, began in the spring of 1979.

In December 1979, the Soviet army invaded Afghanistan with eighty thousand troops. The Communist regime installed by the Soviet invasion survived until April 1992, first under Babrak Karmal (1979-1986) and then under Dr. Najibullah (1986-1992). Following the Soviet invasion in 1979, more than 6 million Afghans fled to the neighboring countries of Pakistan and Iran, among others.[53] It is estimated that more than 1

---

[50] *Id*, at 1.3.

[51] *Id*

[52] *Encyclopedia of the Modern Middle East, Supra,* 45, at p.2.

[53] United Nations High Commission for Refugees. Afghanistan the Unending Crises. *Refugees.* 1997;108:3-9.

million people were killed in Afghanistan before the withdrawal of Soviet troops and the change in government in April, 1992.[54]

After a decade of war, the failure of a Soviet military victory and increasing outside military and financial support of *mujaheddin* ("freedom fighter") forces led to the signing of the Geneva accords on April 14, 1988 under United Nations auspices. The accord called for the withdrawal of Soviet troops, which was completed in February 1989. After the withdrawal of the Soviet troops, Najibulla managed to hold on to power for three more years through continuing support from Moscow. At the same time, several attempts were made to establish a coalition of the political forces in Afghanistan with the Najibullah government, but without success. Najibulla's government collapsed in April 1992 and the *mujaheddin* entered Kabul.

Afghanistan became an Islamic state ruled by a fragmented power structure that was headed by President Burhanuddin Rabbani. The Leadership Council declared Islamic law (*Shari'a*) to be the law of the country. Existing laws considered to be contrary to Islamic law were declared null and void.[55] As various Islamic factions increased their military activities, they soon turned their weapons against each other for control of the capital. Combatants of various factions also engaged in looting, burglary, kidnapping and rape of civilians. Over the next several years, the residents of Kabul suffered tremendous losses. Approximately 50% of Kabul's population fled and most of the city's infrastructure was destroyed in the fighting.

Between 1993-1996, the city of Kabul became a center of heavy shelling and rocketing by forces of Gulbudeen Hekmatyar (and later by the Taliban movement). This led to further killing and disabling of thousands of civilians and extensive destruction of the city. Since 1992, as many as 40,000 civilians have been killed in Kabul when the Communist regime fell and violent power struggles erupted among various *mujaheddin* groups.[56] The power struggle for Kabul between various factions displaced over 500,000 people in 1992.

In November 1994, a new group named "Taliban" emerged as a military and political force. Taliban, which means "students of Muslim religions studies," are poorly educated rural Pashtun youths who were mostly recruited from refugee camps and religious schools ("*madrasas*") in neighboring Pakistan. This movement, led by Mullah

---

[54] *E/CN.4/1996/64, Supra,29*

[55] *DHA Report, Supra,* 1, at 1.5.

[56] US Committee for Refugees. *World Refugee Survey,* 1997. Washington, DC: US Committee for Refugees; 1997:124-125.

Mohammed Omar, a 31-year-old religious leader, claims to be restoring peace and security through the imposition of a strict Islamic order. The emergence of the Taliban movement was greatly facilitated by Pakistan's Inter Services Intelligence Directorate (ISI) and extremist political and religious factions.[57] The Taliban is especially closely linked to the *Jamiat-e Ulema-I Islam* political party of Pakistan, but its sources of support within Pakistan transcend politics. The Taliban has close ties to influential Pakistani businesses — licit and illicit — including the transportation mafia that is based in Peshawar. The imposition of duties on trucks crossing into Afghanistan from Pakistan in the busy smuggling trade between the two countries was and is an essential source of financial support for the Taliban, which controls the routes. And the burgeoning cultivation and transport of opium, notwithstanding Taliban's initial promise to stamp out the drug industry, provides the regime with millions of dollars in revenue.[58]

Over the past twenty years of strife, the Pakistani military and intelligence services (ISI) have played a very large role in Afghanistan. Years before the Taliban emerged, the ISI strongly backed Gulbeddin Hekmatyar, one of the most brutal and conservative of the many *mujaheddin* factions. Gulbeddin's forces (and other factions) received the lion's share of millions of dollars worth of weapons from Pakistan, much of which was provided indirectly by the United States during the Soviet occupation of Afghanistan.[59] When Gulbeddin failed to oust the Rabbani regime after a two-year-long effort to take Kabul (during which time the city was virtually destroyed) the ISI turned its support to the nascent

---

[57] Most of the Taliban are the children of the "*jihad*" against the Soviet Union. Many were born in Pakistani refugee camps, educated in Pakistani *madrasas* and learned their fighting skills from Afghan *mujaheddin* parties based in Pakistan. Their families continued to live in Pakistan as refugees even after the fall of Kabul to the *mujaheddin* in 1992. While all Taliban speak their mother tongue *Pashto*, for many their second language is not Persian, the lingua franca of Afghanistan, but *Urdu*, the language of Pakistan. Ahmed Rashid. "Pakistan and the Taliban," In *Fundamentalism Reborn?, Supra*, 43

[58] *Id.*

[59] The United States provided approximately $2 to $3 billion in military and economic assistance to resistance forces, according to Asia Watch, "Afghanistan, the Forgotten War," 1991. The report cites the following from *Washington Post* correspondent James Rupert: "U.S. officials cited over the years in the *Washington Post*, the *New York Times* and other media gave figures for the annual military aid allocations that, from FY 1980 through FY 1989 equaled about $2.8 billion... This does not include more than $150 million in food, surplus (non-lethal) Defense Department equipment, and transportation assistance given the guerrillas and their supporters under a program administered by the U.S. Agency for International Development." *World Policy Journal*, Vol. VI, No. 4, Fall 1989, pp. 759-785.

Taliban, which was already receiving considerable aid from ethnically, politically, and financially motivated Pashtun circles and from local Pakistani officials. Saudi Arabia also played an important role in backing Gulbeddin (and later, reportedly, the Taliban) and Iran was the patron of the Rabbani government and some Northern Alliance factions.[60]

The government of Prime Minister Benazir Bhutto was reportedly supportive of the Taliban in its rise to power and in September 1994 it dispatched the Interior Minister to work out a settlement between the Taliban and other Afghan warlords.[61] The initiative failed, but Pakistani support for the Taliban continued. Following the Taliban's unexpected capture of Kandahar in November 1994, some 12,000 Pakistani and Afghan students from the *madrasas* in Pakistan joined the Taliban. And Pakistan provided decisive military support when an important munitions dump guarded by Pakistani frontier forces under the Ministry of the Interior was turned over to the Taliban, and with it 18,000 Kalashnikov rifles, 120 artillery units, and large quantities of ammunition.[62]

The capture of Kandahar was followed by Taliban's takeover of other major cities, including Herat in September 1995. In September, Taliban launched an all-out attack on Kabul, subjecting the city to indiscriminate bombing and rocket attacks and killing and wounding thousands of civilians. During the Taliban takeover of Kabul, some 15,000 people, mostly from Kabul, crossed into Pakistan and approximately 180,000 people fled northwards and eastwards.[63] Its first act was an ominous portent: soldiers invaded the United Nations compound and captured and hung former communist president Najibullah and his brother, who had been sheltered there since the communist government fell in 1992.[64]

Notwithstanding official denials from Islamabad, Pakistan's association with Taliban today is undeniable. Pakistan is one of only three countries to formally recognize the Taliban, along with Saudia Arabia

---

[60] *Fundamentalism Reborn?*, *Supra,* 43, "Saudia Arabia, Iran and the Conflict in Afghanistan," by Anwar-ul-Haq Ahady.

[61] *Fundamentalism Reborn.? Supra*, 43, p. 79

[62] Author Ahmed Rashid reported that the Taliban capture of Kandahar in 1994 was "wildly celebrated by the *Jamiat-e Ulema-I Islam* and the Bhutto government, but created an uproar amongst other political parties who felt directly threatened. Mehmood Khan Achakzai, head of the Pushtoonkhwa Milli Awami Party in Baluchistan publicly warned Bhutto and the ISI not to interfere in Afghanistan by trying to promote the Jamiat-e Ulema-i Islam. Other Baluch and *Pashtun* politicians issued similar warnings." *Fundamentalism Reborn?*, *Supra,* 43, p. 81.

[63] Statement by the UN Under-Secretary-General, Nov. 1996

[64] *Afghanistan: Grave Abuses in the Name of Religion*, Amnesty International, November 1996.

and the United Arab Emirates. In 1996, 26 Pakistani fighters, recruited by the Pakistani ISI to help the Taliban in its drive on Kabul, were captured by then-government forces and held in prison in Panjshir city. The men provided detailed information on the ISI's assistance to the Taliban, including the recruitment and training of Pakistani troops, and provision of vehicles, weapons, and money.[65] Several inhabitants of Kabul confirmed the existence of some buildings, such as the former Cuban embassy, as occupied by Pakistani citizens working with the Taliban administration.

While fighting has continued between opposing Afghan forces, the political situation in Afghanistan has remain unchanged. The Taliban control the capital of Kabul and the predominantly Pashtun-populated regions of the country, while the Northern Alliance control their respective areas from Mazar-I-Sharif, Taluqan and Bamyan. Also, the six constituent parties of the Northern Alliance continued their efforts to form a more coherent political grouping under the name "United Islamic and National Front for the Salvation of Afghanistan" (UNIFSA).

Anti-Taliban forces affiliated with the Northern Alliance are responsible for indiscriminate bombardment and rocketing of civilian areas. Since the Taliban takeover of Kabul, anti-Taliban forces have occasionally rocketed strategic installations in and around Kabul. General Dostam's warplanes bombed Taliban facilities in Kabul in January 1997. General Masood's forces have rocketed the military-civilian airport in Kabul since the spring of 1998. It is reported that in these rocket attacks, some civilians have been killed or injured in the vicinity of these installations.

In 1997, the International Committee of the Red Cross (ICRC) reported that the number of direct victims of the conflict had risen sharply since the beginning of that year. Fighting in the north of Kabul, for example, had resulted in a total of 200,000 people displaced. According to an ICRC report, the death rate among war casualties in districts north of the capital was alarmingly high in 1997, with one out of every two to three casualties resulting in death.

In addition, Afghanistan is the most densely mined country in the world. It is estimated that the country has 10 per cent of the estimated 100 million mines laid in 64 countries of the world.[66] As many as 10 million landmines remain in Afghanistan[67] and, as of November 1997, the

---

[65] "Friends of the Taliban, As fighting nears Kabul, two POW's tell TIME that Pakistan sent soldiers to help the extreme Islamists." *Time Magazine*, November 4, 1996.

[66] *E/CN.4/1996/64, Supra*,29.

[67] *Id.*

current known area still contaminated by landmines is 725,000 square kilometers. It is estimated that since 1992, landmines have killed more than 20,000 people and injured more than 400,000 others in Afghanistan.[68] Approximately 80% of the landmine casualties are civilian and among these, 40-50% are women and children.[69]

The Taliban, rejecting the opposition's claim to be the legal government of Afghanistan, continue efforts to gain international recognition through the dispatch of delegations to Japan, the Republic of Korea, China and Thailand. The reality remains, however, that Afghanistan remains in a civil war without an effective government and its people continue to suffer the consequences.

The United Nations and organizations such as the International Committee of the Red Cross (ICRC) have repeatedly worked to bring the warring factions to a dialogue for peace, but without success. Regional powers involved in the Afghan civil war have the ability to end the conflict, but they have failed to do so. According to Ralph Magnus, Coordinator of Middle East Area Studies in the Department of National Security, Naval Postgraduate School, Monterey, CA, "They enthusiastically proclaim their support for UN peace efforts, but they fan the fires of conflict by pouring arms, money and supplies to their preferred Afghan factions."[70]

Regional countries bordering Afghanistan (Pakistan, Iran, Turkmenistan, Uzbekistan, Tajikistan and China) plus the United States and Russia, in the so-called "Six Plus Two Peace Process," began a peace initiative in October 1997. These discussions started after the victory of Mohammed Khatami in the Iranian presidential election and the appointment of Kamal Kharrazi, Iranian former UN representative, as foreign minister. At the same time, bilateral discussions between Pakistani and Iranian representatives took place throughout the year in 1997. Thus far, peace negotiations have not ended the conflict.

For the past year, another initiative involving groups of ex-patriate Afghans has been started to help resolve the crisis through a *loya jirga* (grand assembly) The *jirga*, has been endorsed by the anti-Taliban alliance, however, the Taliban have thus far refused to attend any of the preliminary meetings. The group held initial meetings in Frankfurt, Istanbul, and, most recently, in Bonn, Germany. The Bonn meeting, held in July 1998, gathered approximately 150 Afghans representing almost all ethnic, political, and social communities, except the Taliban. As part of this new initiative, it was decided to encourage the Taliban to participate through future dialogue.

---

[68] *Id.*

[69] *Country Report on Human Rights, Supra,* 3.

[70] See Magnus R H, Afghanistan in 1997: The War Moves North, *Asian Survey* (University of California Press 1998).

Today, under the Taliban, there is no Constitution, rule of law, or independent judiciary in Afghanistan. In the absence of an independent judiciary, many municipal and provincial authorities use the Taliban's interpretation of *Shari'a* and traditional tribal codes of justice.[71] The Taliban reportedly have Islamic courts in areas under their control to judge criminal cases and resolve disputes. These courts mete out punishments including execution and amputations. In cases involving murder and rape, convicted prisoners generally are sentenced to execution by relatives of the victim, who may instead choose to accept other forms of restitution. Decisions of the courts are reportedly final.

The government of former President Burhanuddin Rabbani still retains Afghanistan's UN seat.[72] Taliban officials have tried unsuccessfully to gain the UN seat for Afghanistan as they control more than two third of the country.

In October 1997, the Taliban changed the name of the country to the Islamic Emirate of Afghanistan with Mullah Omar, who had previously assumed the religious title of Emir of the Faithful, as the supreme head of state. Taliban officials rule by decrees and the central decision-making body is the Supreme Council in Kandahar and its head, Mullah Mohammed Omar. A six-member ruling council in Kabul, headed by Mullah Mohammed Rabbani, has announced that "the new Taliban government would be neither parliamentary nor presidential, but Islamic."[73] Departments of a number of ministries exist in each province but the implementation of policy is generally characterized by inconsistency since there is no efficient administrative structure.

Nearly 20 years of war, political instability and lack of a legitimate and functional government have devastated Afghanistan's economy and severely restricted job opportunities. The economy of Afghanistan suffers from near total destruction of the nation's industrial infrastructure, soaring inflation, the lack of banking and communication systems, and more recently, the Taliban's exclusion of women from the work force.

Industrial production fell from 38 billion Afghanis in 1987 to 30 billion in 1992 resulting in 45% of the workforce losing their jobs. Agricultural production fell from 90 billion Afghanis in 1987 to 60 billion in 1992. The health care and education infrastructure has been virtually destroyed by war and "brain drain" of more than 100,000 of the country's educated and technically trained elite who have resettled abroad.[74]

---

[71] *DHA Report, Supra,* 1, at 2.1.

[72] *Country Report on Human Rights, Supra, 3.*

[73] *DHA Report, Supra,* 1, at 3.5.

[74] Refugee Policy Group Resource Paper, *Afghanistan: Policy and Operational Responses to Relief, Rehabilitation and Reconstruction.* November 1996, p. 3

Unemployment has been rising steadily. In Kabul, over 80 percent of the population is unemployed. Furthermore, workers in government ministries reportedly have been fired because they received part of their education abroad, because of contacts with the previous regimes, or because of insufficient beard length.[75] Most government offices and the private sector are non-functional. The number of street beggars in Kabul has increased at an alarming rate. For most Kabul residents (widows, children, men and women without a source of income) begging has become a new way of survival. In addition, more than half of Afghanistan's housing was damaged or destroyed in the war.

Historically, Afghanistan's predominant economic activity has been agriculture. Although opium traditionally has been grown in Afghanistan, in recent years, opium cultivation has become the principal economic activity in Afghanistan.[76] The current production of dry opium – estimated at more than 2,200 metric tons a year - reportedly equals the combined production of the other three biggest opium producers in the world, with important consequences for the global consumption of heroin. At present, the Taliban controls 95% of the opium-producing land in Afghanistan.

Oil Companies and the Taliban

Recently, the oil companies in the United States and other countries have turned their attention to Afghanistan in efforts to gain access to the more than 200 billion barrels of oil in central Asia. Three major oil companies have planned construction of a 1,040 mile-long oil pipeline. The pipeline would begin in Turkmenistan and extend through Afghanistan and Pakistan to the Arabian Sea. Two competing consortiums, one led by Bridas of Argentina and the other a joint project between UNOCAL of the United States and its partner Delta Oil of Saudi Arabia, have been trying to bring the warring factions together in a "pipeline council" to initiate a peace process.[77] UNOCAL representatives have met with Taliban and the Northern Alliance representatives to negotiate the logistics. To date, there is no contract between any of the factions in Afghanistan and UNOCAL. The estimated cost of this project is US $2.5 billion.

---

[75] The Taliban have decreed that men must maintain beards that are longer than a clenched fist clenched at the base of the chin. Non-compliance is often punished by beating, torture and/or imprisonment. See *E/CN.4/1997/59, Supra,* 22

[76] *Id.*

[77] Rashid A, Taliban Rule: Oil companies woo Kabul's new masters, *Far Eastern Economic Review*, April 10, 1997.

In addition, construction of a 790-mile-long natural gas pipeline has been planned. It would originate from the Turkmenistan-Afghanistan border and extend through Afghanistan to Multan in central Pakistan. If implemented, both pipelines will generate annual revenues to the Taliban estimated at US $50-100 million. The Taliban controls the regions that the pipeline would run though in Afghanistan.

Also, Bridas oil company is planing to build a 1,300-kilometer gas pipeline from Yashlar, crossing southern Afghanistan via Herat and Kandahar to Sui in central Pakistan, where the country's gas pipeline network originates. In March 1997, the Taliban allowed Bridas to set up an office in Kabul and UNOCAL to establish an office and training center in Kandahar for pipeline technicians. UNOCAL has been playing a more active role in lobbying both the U.S. State Department and Congress for a solution to the Afghan crisis. According to a senior UN official "the outside interference in Afghanistan is now all related to the battle for oil and gas pipelines. The fear is that these companies and regional powers are just renting the Taliban for their own purposes."[78] UN officials and Afghan community leaders have publicly criticized the oil companies for the "criminalization of the Afghan economy" through their support of the Taliban.[79]

The Status of Women in Afghanistan

Male Afghan leaders have publicly acknowledged the need for reform on the status of women for the past one hundred years. At the end of the 19th century, Amir Abdur Rahman introduced a series of laws in an attempt to align customary social practices with the prescriptions of Islam. Using the dictates of the *Qur'an*, he prohibited child marriages, forced marriages, exorbitant bride prices and marriage gifts, and ruled that women could seek divorce.[80]

Constitutions from 1923 onwards guaranteed equal rights for men and women. Women were automatically enfranchised by the 1964 Constitution which guaranteed all Afghans "dignity, compulsory education and freedom to work."[81] Article 27 of the 1977 Constitution stated, "The entire people of Afghanistan, women and men, without discrimination have equal rights and obligations before the law."[82]

---

[78] *Id*, at p. 33.

[79] *Id*.

[80] Dupree, N. *Afghan Women in the Context of International Women Rights Instruments*, Proceedings of the Seminar: Women's Human Rights in Afghanistan (Mazar-I-Sharif, Afghanistan 1994), pp 14-28.

[81] *Id*, at p. 23.

In 1959, new policies called for expanded roles for women regarding education and career opportunities, the voluntary removal of the veil and the end to the expectation that women should remain in their homes. In 1964, Afghanistan recognized the right of women to vote. Education and work opportunities for women were concentrated primarily in urban areas. By the late 1970s, women students outnumbered male students in Kabul. The progress of modern development in Afghanistan was measured by the emancipation of the Afghan woman and the attraction such policies would exert on rural populations. The status of the women embodied the pride of the urban elite and the bitterness of rural women.

During the 1980s, the Communist government legally ensured equal rights of women with men. Over subsequent years, increasing numbers of educated women worked in government and business, in industry, as hairdressers and diplomats, in the police and in the army, as entertainers and parliamentarians. No career was closed to them. Attitudes toward the role of women changed dramatically as education for girls and employment in public areas for women became more and more acceptable to wider segments of society.

The status of Afghan women changed in April 1992 when the Islamic State of Afghanistan was installed in Kabul.[83] Women were instructed to cover their heads, legs and arms and to observe a strict interpretation of Islamic law regarding the *hijab* (modest clothing). Following the Islamic Government's decree on *hijab*, women continued their activities in the workforce, schools and universities. Shortly after *mujaheddin* forces gained control of Kabul, many atrocities such as forced marriages, kidnapping, rape and torture against women were reported.[84] By 1993, such reports had diminished, but armed conflict between various factions continued in the city.

Since mid-1994, the status of women shifted dramatically in areas under Taliban control. Soon after the Taliban took control of Kabul in September 1996, the Supreme Council issued edicts[85] forbidding women to work outside the home, attend school, or to leave their homes unless accompanied by a *mahram* (husband, father, brother, or son). In public, women must be covered from head to toe in a "*burqa*," with only a mesh opening to see and breathe through. They are not permitted to wear white (the color of the Taliban flag) socks or white shoes, or shoes that make noise as they walk. Houses and buildings in public view must have their

---

[82] *Id.*

[83] *Id*, at p. 24.

[84] Amnesty International, *Afghanistan : A Human Rights Catastrophe*, Amnesty International,1995.

[85] See Appendices A, B, and C.

windows painted over if females are present. They are not permitted to be examined by a male health worker in the absence of a male chaperone. And they are largely prohibited from working, resulting in the brutal impoverishment of their families, especially the enormous number of families who have lost a male breadwinner as a casualty of war.

Also, the Taliban severely limited women's access to health care and closed public bath houses for women. Initially, these edicts were enforced in a haphazard manner, and varied from region to region, with more severe restrictions enforced in non-Pashtun areas.

Human Rights Violations and the Taliban

The people of Afghanistan have suffered extensive human rights violations in the course of the past twenty years. The Soviet invasion and occupation from 1979 to 1989, aided by Afghan communist military and civilian collaborators, brought mass killings, torture, disappearance, the largest recorded refugee outflow in history, and a scourge of landmines. The civil war, fueled by regional countries' support for various factions following the collapse of the Soviet-backed regime in 1992, witnessed extensive abuses by the various armed factions vying for power, including the virtual destruction of Kabul from rocket shelling, aerial bombardment and mortaring. Indiscriminate use of force, torture and killing in detention of both civilians and combatants, the laying of antipersonnel landmines, and the arbitrary exercise of authority principally through military force characterized Afghanistan for much of this period.

But as dire as the human rights situation has been, the Taliban regime, which rose to power beginning in 1994 and today controls two-thirds of Afghanistan, has brought the country to a new level of desperation and horror. The Taliban has imposed strict Islamic sanctions for common crimes and regularly carries out floggings, executions (including by beheading or stoning) and amputations, which the public is summoned to watch. Taliban soldiers engage in violations of humanitarian law in the continuing civil war, including massacres of civilians and deliberate or indiscriminate rocketing of villages or towns held by opposing forces.[86] Due process is absent; the Taliban's *Shari'a* courts operate arbitrarily, and authority is maintained through tyranny and terror.

PHR gained firsthand knowledge of those experiences while in Kabul.[87] Every Friday, the Taliban terrorizes the city of Kabul by publicly punishing

---

[86] Amnesty International, *Flagrant Abuse, Supra*,13.

alleged wrongdoers in the Kabul sports stadium and requiring public attendance at the floggings, shootings, hangings, beheadings, and amputations.[88] On one occasion, PHR's researcher witnessed the public execution (stabbing and beheading) of two men convicted of murder by the Taliban *Shari'a* court at the sports stadium. On another day, the researcher witnessed the amputation of an alleged thief's hand and the flogging of an eighteen-year-old girl who was accused of having an affair. The researcher said that before, during, and after the execution and punishments, the stadium was filled with women and children crying and pleading with the authorities and the executioners not to carry out the sentences, albeit in vain.[89]

But the aspect of Taliban rule that most deeply affects the life of women is the Taliban's idiosyncratic interpretation of the holy *Qur'an* with regard to the role of women.[90] Their interpretation of *Shari'a* forbids women to work outside the home, attend school, or leave their homes unless accompanied by a husband, father, brother, or son.

The Taliban's abuses are by no means limited to women. Thousands of men have been taken prisoner, arbitrarily detained, tortured, and many killed and disappeared. Men are beaten and jailed for not wearing beards of sufficient length (that of a clenched fist beneath the chin), are subjected to cruel and degrading conditions in jail, and suffer such pun-

---

[87] The organization's researcher herself narrowly escaped a beating when she was pursued by a young member of the security forces brandishing a whip, as he screamed at her for exposing her wrists and for being alone in public.

[88] Amnesty International reported on March 13, 1998: over 30,000 spectators made up of women and boys were summoned by loudspeaker to gather at Kabul's sports stadium to watch the father and brother of a murdered man shoot an alleged murderer who had been sentenced to death by a Taliban *Shari'a* court. *Flagrant Abuse Supra*, 13.

[89] The researcher saw a number of women who were apparently family members on the field at the execution site. The executions were carried out in front of them; following the beheadings, the women, shrouded in *burqas*, continued crouching next to the bodies.

[90] Physicians for Human Rights relies upon international humanitarian and human rights law as its standards for judging the human rights record of every country on which it reports, and does not engage in disputes over interpretations of religious works. It is worth noting, however, that there is no place within the *Qur'an* where discrimination against women in health or education is promoted or justified. See Chapter VI.

[91] Physicians for Human Rights obtained first-hand information about two cases of gang rape of boys by Taliban police. One was thirteen, the other eighteen years old. The thirteen-year-old child had been abducted following a fight he had with the son of a Taliban supporter. In prison he was reportedly beaten and raped by Taliban security forces. The eighteen-year-old had been held for eight days during which time he was reportedly repeatedly raped by Taliban security forces; He reported having emotional problems and physical injuries as a consequence of this abuse. Both of the boys are Hazara, who are particularly vulnerable to Taliban depredations.

ishments as amputation and stoning. Men are also vulnerable to extortion, arrest, gang rape,[91] and abuse in detention because of their ethnicity or presumed political views.[92] The Taliban's *Shari'a* courts lack even a semblance of due process, with no provisions for legal counsel and frequent use of torture to extract confessions.[93]

The Taliban is not the only party within Afghanistan to have committed abuses of human rights. Grave violations of the laws of armed conflict are committed in varying degree by different factions of the Northern Alliance, which retain control of approximately one-third of the country, principally in the area of Mazar-I-Sharif. Indeed, it was during the struggle for power between the Rabbani government and Gulbeddin Hekmatyar and other factions which reduced Kabul to rubble during the civil war period of 1992 to 1995 and caused literally thousands of civilian casualties. That period also witnessed rampant human rights abuses by the warring parties before Taliban was on the scene: rape was rampant, torture, killings, disappearances, and arbitrary arrest common.

Today, the anti-Taliban alliance has targeted military and civilian airports in Kabul and inflicted casualties on civilians living nearby. The group is said to be laying new landmines. The northern portion of Afghanistan controlled by various opposition factions is almost inaccessible to relief workers, due to ubiquitous extortion, killings, and theft.

In December 1997, a team from the United Nations High Commissioner for Human Rights led by Professor Choong-Hyun Paik, Special Rapporteur on Human Rights for Afghanistan, and which included a forensic anthropologist from Physicians for Human Rights, investigated five alleged grave sites in northern Afghanistan, said to contain hundreds of Taliban prisoners executed in the summer or fall of 1997. Of the five sites evaluated, three showed evidence consistent with informants' accounts of prisoners being taken out and executed: The Nine Wells Site, the Hairatan Highway Desert Site, and the Ridge Site. Physicians for Human Rights found evidence that suggests over 100 bodies at the sites and has requested the UN to continue the investigation.[94]

---

[92] Shiite men or men of Hazara or Tajik ethnicity are presumed to support the opposition Northern Alliance.

[93] In April 1998, Amnesty International reported: "In recent months, at least five men convicted of sodomy [presumed to be homosexuals] by Taliban *Shari'a* courts have been placed next to standing walls by Taliban officials and then buried under the rubble as the walls were toppled upon them. At least four alleged murderers have been executed in public by the family members of the murdered persons. At least five men have had their hands amputated on allegation of theft, and at least one man and one woman have been flogged by Taliban officials on allegation of adultery *Flagrant Abuse, Supra*,13.

The Taliban is, however, the first faction laying claim to power in Afghanistan which has targeted women for extreme repression and punished them brutally for infractions. To our knowledge, no other regime in the world has methodically and violently forced half of its population into virtual house arrest, prohibiting them on pain or physical punishment from showing their faces, seeking medical care without a male escort, or attending school.

It is also difficult to find another government or would-be government in the world that has deliberately created such poverty by arbitrarily depriving half the population under its control of jobs, schooling, mobility, and health care. Such restrictions are literally life threatening to women and to their children. PHR's researcher when visiting Kabul in 1998 saw a city of beggars — women who had once been teachers and nurses now moving in the streets like ghosts under their enveloping *burqas*, selling every possession and begging so as to feed their children.

United States Strategic Interests and Policy

The United States has been heavily involved in Afghanistan since the invasion of the country by the Soviet Union in 1979. Approximately $2 to $3 billion in economic and military aid to various *mujaheddin* factions was funneled by the U.S. through Pakistani military and intelligence agencies, notably the ISI. Among the chief beneficiaries was the *Hezb-e Islami* force, headed by Gulbeddin Hekmatyar and responsible for some of the worst atrocities of the civil war. Despite the fact that the U.S. was clearly aware of extensive human rights violations by factions it aided, there is no evidence that any action was taken by the U.S. to prohibit Pakistan from distributing aid to the worst of the resistance forces or to criticize the Pakistani ISI for itself participating in abuses.[95]

The U.S. continued to fund the *mujaheddin* factions after the Soviet withdrawal when civil war between the factions engulfed the country. This policy of helping fund a military victory over the Soviet-backed Najibullah regime was apparently controversial even within the Bush Administration. Asia Watch (now Human Rights Watch/Asia) reported that Robert Kimmitt, Undersecretary of State for Political Affairs, was engaged in a battle with the CIA, which was hoping for a guerrilla win in Afghanistan. Kimmitt was said to prefer working with Moscow to encourage the Najibullah regime into holding democratic elections. Kim-

---

[94] *Human Remains from Alleged Mass Graves in Northern Afghanistan*, by Mark Skinner, Ph.D., D.A.B.F.A., Physicians for Human Rights consultant, submitted to the UN High Commissioner for Human Rights on January 6, 1998.

[95] *Afghanistan, the Forgotten War*, Asia Watch, 1991, at p. 129.

mitt even went so far as to publicly accuse the CIA of pursuing its own military agenda: "If they [the CIA] have a problem at the agency it is with me carrying out a policy that has been set down by the Secretary and reaffirmed by the President during the June summit... I have no hesitation in saying that their problem is not with me but with the senior leadership of this department and this government. I think they are just bucking policy."[96]

By early 1992, Washington's support for the insurgents had ended and by April, the *mujaheddin* had entered Kabul. Some observers have characterized the period of 1992 to 1994 as one of drift and neglect of Afghanistan by the U.S. Indeed, policy makers professed to be unaware about the rise of the Taliban during this period.[97]

Following the Taliban's capture of Kandahar, the U.S. appeared to be supportive of the faction for several reasons. The group's initial professed intention to clean up the drug trade was of interest, as was its anti-Iran stance. Perhaps most importantly, the Taliban appeared to be the faction most likely to provide security for an oil and gas pipeline project proposed by the U.S. petroleum company, UNOCAL.[98] UNOCAL officials themselves applauded the fall of Kabul to the Taliban and expressed their eagerness to do business with the regime.

The U.S. position during the Taliban's early years may be seen in the remarks of the Assistant Secretary of State for South Asian Affairs, Ms. Robin Raphel, in a statement at a November 1996 United Nations meeting:

Despite nearly universal misgivings about the Taliban, it must be acknowledged as a significant factor in the Afghan equation and one that will not simply disappear any time soon. The Taliban control more than two-thirds of the country; they are Afghan, they are indigenous, they have demonstrated staying power. The reasons they have succeeded so far have little to do with military prowess or outside military assistance. Indeed, when they have engaged in truly serious fighting, the Taliban have not fared so well. The real

---

[96] Clifford Kraus, Hot Spots Like the Gulf, He's Baker's Cool Hand, *New York Times*, January 3, 1991. Cited in *Afghanistan, the Forgotten War*, Asia Watch, 1991 at p. 127.

[97] As Barnett R. Rubin noted in a paper for *Muslim Politics Report*, a publication of the Council on Foreign Relations, the entire international community had no political strategy for Afghanistan from 1992 to 1994... At that time, the evolution of the Taliban was underway... At the time, American officials professed general ignorance of the identity and origin of the group, obfuscating any suggestion that the Taliban were financed and backed by Pakistan — a U.S. position that today appears ludicrous." Richard Mackenzie, "The United States and the Taliban," in *Fundamentalism Reborn?*, *Supra*, 43,at p. 95.

[98] *Id*, at 97.

source of their success has been the willingness of many Afghans, particularly Pashtuns, to tacitly trade unending fighting and chaos for a measure of peace and security, even with severe social restrictions. We must all recognize that the Afghan people, after having been battered by relentless fighting and unrest for 17 years, are war-weary and tired of the factional fighting. The people seem eager for peace at almost any price.[99]

This notion that the Taliban offered peace and that the Afghan people welcomed it, notwithstanding its price, is a durable, albeit flawed analysis of Afghanistan under the Taliban. As PHR's health and human rights survey of women indicates, this is not an analysis shared by Afghan women themselves.[100] Women were overwhelmingly horrified by the Taliban and its repressive rule, and many indicated that the period of civil war and rocketing was preferable to a life of begging, hunger, virtual house arrest, imprisonment, and enforced wearing of the *burqa*. Moreover, Raphel's insistence that the Taliban is "indigenous" and the implication that it achieved power because of popular support is surprising, given the clear record of military, economic, and political support provided by Pakistan.

As Taliban consolidated their control, their gross abuses, particularly against women, and failure to make good on promises to crack down on the drug trade, their glow appeared to fade in Washington.[101] The Taliban's close association with the Saudi billionaire Osama bin Laden, whom American intelligence agencies believed was involved in the terrorist attack on an American barracks in Saudi Arabia, further soured Washington on the Taliban.[102]

With Madeleine Albright's appointment as Secretary of State in 1997 and the replacement of Raphel with Ambassador Karl (Rick) Inderfurth, U.S. criticism of the Taliban accelerated. Secretary Albright's visit to an Afghan refugee camp in November 1997 and her strong speech condemning Taliban's abuses of women and children were a clear break with past American policy. The Secretary not only championed the rights of women and girls but went on to say that "... we do not believe that the Taliban are in a position to occupy all of Afghanistan."

---

[99] Statement by Robin L. Raphel, Head of U.S. Delegation, United Nations Meeting on Afghanistan, November 18, 1996.

[100] See Chapter III.

[101] As reported by Richard Mackenzie, far from ending the trade, the production and transport of opium accelerated in areas under Taliban control. *Fundamentalism Reborn?, Supra*, 43, at 100.

[102] *Id.*

At a Congressional hearing in October 1997, Assistant Secretary of State Inderfurth stated: "Let me be very clear about our policy toward Afghanistan. The U.S. is neutral between the factions. We want only a peaceful, stable, united, and independent Afghanistan that neither is threatened by nor is a threat to its neighbors... In the long term, we would like to see emerge an Afghan government that is multi-ethnic, broad-based, and that observes international norms of behavior."[103]

Humanitarian Assistance in Afghanistan

Afghanistan is one of the poorest countries in the world. It has one of the highest infant (165/1000) and child (257/1000) mortality rates of all countries.[104] Life expectancy at birth is 45 years.[105] Access to safe drinking water in rural areas is 5% and in urban areas 39%,[106] and it is estimated that 42% of all deaths in Afghanistan are due to diarrheal diseases.[107] Malnutrition affects up to 35% of children under age 5,[108] and 85,000 children under age five die annually from diarrheal diseases.[109]

Afghans remain the United Nations High Commissioner for Refugees' largest single caseload of refugees in the world for the 17th year in succession.[110] In 1996, there were 2.7 million Afghans remaining outside Afghanistan, 1.4 million in Iran and 1.2 million in Pakistan.[111] Women and children constitute three quarters of the refugee population. Also, as many as 1.2 million Afghans were thought to be internally displaced at the end of 1996.[112]

The civilian population of Afghanistan is almost wholly dependent upon the sustenance of the international aid community. Seventy percent

---

[103] Statement of Ambassador Karl Inderfurth, Senate Foreign Relations Subcommittee on Asia and the Pacific, October 22, 1997.

[104] United Nations Children's Fund. *State of the World's Children Report*, 1997. New York, NY: United Nations Children's Fund; 1997.

[105] *Id.*

[106] United Nations Development Program. *Human Development Report, 1997.* New York, NY: Oxford University Press; 1997.

[107] *E/CN.4/1996/64, Supra,* 29

[108] UNICEF/CIET Multiple Indicator Cluster Survey; 1997:2-26.

[109] *DHA Report, Supra,*1.

[110] United Nations High Commissioner for Refugees. Focus: Afghanistan the Unending Crises. *Refugees.* 1997;108:3-9.

[111] *Id.*; and *E/CN.4/1996/64, Supra,* 29.

[112] *Id.*

[113] World Health Organization. *Hope.* Geneva, Switzerland: World Health Organization. December, 1996.

of the health care system in Afghanistan is dependent on external assistance.[113] United Nations' humanitarian agencies report feeding hundreds of thousands of Afghans, and subsidized bread sales reportedly reach over one million. International aid represents a significant component of national economy, given the wholesale destruction of indigenous production and markets. With one of the highest infant mortality rates in the world, a health infrastructure in tatters, tens of thousands of war widows, and epidemic numbers of landmine injuries, the provision of humanitarian assistance to Afghanistan is a moral imperative.But the Taliban's policy of extreme segregation of women and girls make it almost impossible for donor governments and humanitarian aid agencies to carry out respectable programs which reach those most in need.

There are currently more than 40 international non-governmental organizations (NGOs) in addition to national governmental and United Nations agencies active in Afghanistan. Most of these organizations have focused on assisting vulnerable groups, with many development, health, and food distribution programs targeting women and their families. The increased limits on women's activities imposed by the Taliban regime have constrained program efforts to benefit women beyond the distribution of food and basic supplies. In response, some NGOs, such as Save the Children-UK, which focused on education and health[114] temporarily closed operations in Taliban-controlled areas. In 1996, United Nations agencies, following the lead of UNICEF, also stopped support for school education programs in areas of Afghanistan where governmental decrees denied girls access to schooling.[115]

International agencies have struggled, accordingly, to continue seeking means to address the needs of Afghan women in the context of the Taliban regime's discriminatory, gender-based policies. How best to achieve this has been at the center of debate both within and among the international organizations working in Afghanistan.[116] The international aid community is divided over the question of whether or how best to provide humanitarian assistance to Afghanistan under Taliban rule. For

---

[114] United Nations, *Afghanistan: An Enduring Tragedy*, Department of Humanitarian Affairs, May 1996, p. 5.

[115] *Id.*

[116] DHA Report, *Supra*,1,for a full discussion of different United Nations agencies' divergent strategies for reconciling their program goals of supporting women's livelihoods and training with Taliban decrees.

[117] See *Agence France Presse*, July 24, 1998 (www.afghanradio.com). Ms. Bonino was arrested by the Taliban and detained for several hours along with her entourage, some of whom were beaten, because she met with Afghan women during her visit to Kabul on September 29, 1998.

example, Emma Bonino, the European Commissioner for Human Rights, has called for the suspension of all United Nations assistance.[117]

Recurring problems with the security of its employees, including the physical assault on its representative in Kandahar by Taliban militants, led to a withdrawal of the UN from Kandahar in April, 1998. Some within the United Nations were privately suggesting that all international assistance be limited to life-sustaining, emergency assistance: water, food, and vaccinations. A negotiating team under the auspices of the United Nations Office for the Coordination of Humanitarian Affairs and the Special Mission for Afghanistan was dispatched to Kabul in May 1998, and a ten-day long negotiation ensued.

On May 13, a Memorandum of Understanding (MOU) was agreed upon and signed between the UN and the Taliban. The MOU appears to have met the UN's concerns over the security of its staff and operations, containing numerous commitments by the Taliban as to the inviolability of UN vehicles, property, communication and transportation and immunity from prosecution for the UN's international and national staff. The Taliban agreed as well that the United Nations "shall be free to employ staff without distinction based on race, gender, religion, or nationality, in accordance with its policies and criteria and with due respect to Islamic traditions."[118] The UN, for its part, agreed to refrain from political activities and religious proselytism and to pay "proper respect" to Islamic principles and local customs.

With regard to women's access to health and education, however, the UN appeared to have gained little, if anything at all, notwithstanding the boast made by Under Secretary General for Humanitarian Affairs Sergio Vieira de Mello in a May 15 memorandum accompanying the MOU that said that "critical progress has been made on ... access to health and education for women and girls."

The text of the MOU itself actually states something very different. Article 12 and 13 appear to commit the United Nations to the Taliban's view of Islamic law, Afghan culture, and the rights of women.

Article 12 states: "The Islamic Emirate of Afghanistan and United Nations jointly commit that men and women shall have the right to education and health care and necessary development activities, based on international standards and in accordance with Islamic rules and Afghan culture." Article 13 states: "The Authorities and the UN will make efforts to increase the participation of men and women in health, education — especially health education — and food security. Both parties acknowledge the economic difficulties and the specific cultural tradi-

---

[118] Memorandum of Understanding Between the Islamic Emirate of Afghanistan and the United Nations, May 13, 1998.

tions that make this goal challenging. As a result, women's access to and participation in health and education will need to be gradual."

The MOU also addresses the question of international female Muslim staff of the UN who are not accompanied by male escorts. Article 11 states that "The Islamic Emirate of Afghanistan is ready to discuss with religious scholars from Islamic countries the movement of international female Muslim staff of the UN who are not accompanied by *Mahram* [male minders] in order to reach a solution in accordance with *Shari'a*. It is believed that this issue will be resolved in the near future."[119]

The United Nations' conferring of its imprimatur on the Taliban's unique interpretation of Afghan religion and culture, its explicit endorsement of the notion that segregation from health and education facilities is integral to Afghan history and culture, its agreeing that restitution of services must be "gradual," and its deference to Islamic religious scholars on the question of whether its own female staff may work independently in Afghanistan, are a grave disservice to the women of Afghanistan and to the UN's own female staff.[120]

The MOU is even more troubling when read in light of a confidential memorandum by Martin Griffith, a diplomat from the United Nations Special Mission for Afghanistan, which was circulated by the UN as an attachment to the Memorandum of Understanding. Mr. Griffith describes the ten-day negotiations with the Taliban and notes that: "The failure or suspension of the Peace Talks in Islamabad occurred just as we were moving to Kabul. We soon realised that, whereas this was in itself a great pity, it would probably make the Taliban keener to come to agreement with us. Indeed, it was clear that were we to come to an agreement with the Taliban, it would probably have more to do with their concern over their international profile than with their desire for UN assistance."

As Mr. Griffith's analysis makes clear, the international community does appear to have some leverage with the Taliban through its presence in the country and the regime's desire to be Afghanistan's representative and interlocutor with the United Nations. Accordingly, it is incumbent upon the United Nations to rescind Articles 11, 12, and 13 of the MOU and convene immediate negotiations to reconsider those portions.

If the United Nations is unable to persuade the Taliban to accept immediate access to education and health care and the ability of female staff (both local and international) to work without male chaperones, then the UN should announce that it is withdrawing all of its staff from

---

[119] *Id.*

[120] Bad Bargain in Afghanistan. *New York Times*. July 14, 1998.

Afghanistan. Until such time as women's rights have been restored fully, international aid to areas controlled by the Taliban should be limited to humanitarian programs: demining, vaccinations, water, and food. Such programs, which may be financed by the United Nations, should be administered by the non-governmental humanitarian agencies.[121]

The Taliban in recent months has demonstrated its contempt for the international community and its increasing hostility to humanitarian organizations attempting to operate within the country. On June 30, 1998, the Taliban issued an edict requiring foreign aid workers to leave their homes in the diplomatic area of the country and reestablish themselves in an isolated dormitory on the outskirts of Kabul with neither water nor power. On July 20, 1998, all foreign aid workers withdrew from Kabul rather than take up residence in unacceptable living quarters.[122]

---

[121] Currently the United Nations maintains only a small staff within Afghanistan. The bulk of UN-funded programs in Afghanistan is already carried out by humanitarian organizations under contract with the international body.

[122] Associated Press, July 20 1998.

III. WOMEN'S HEALTH AND HUMAN RIGHTS SURVEY [123]

Methods [124]

Subjects

Subjects consisted of female heads of household who had lived in Kabul at least two years before September 1996. Active supporters of the Taliban movement and wives of Taliban officials were excluded, since they posed a potential threat to the safety of study participants and the completion of the study. There were no active supporters of opposition groups among study participants.

Names and addresses of women living in Kabul were randomly selected from comprehensive lists of names of clients from four humanitarian service organizations that either assessed communities for possible assistance and/or provided assistance. Of the 57 women selected and asked to participate, 54 completed the survey. Of the three interviews not completed, two were excluded because of their Taliban affiliation and one refused for fear of retaliation. An additional 26 participants from Kabul were obtained through chain (or snowball) sampling [125] of women associated with the humanitarian service organizations. Chain sampling consisted of identifying initial participants through humanitarian assistance organizations, then identifying additional cases from the participants.

In Pakistan, 19 participants were women living in one of two refugee camps and were randomly selected from comprehensive lists of names maintained by refugee organizations. An additional 61 participating

---

[123] This chapter is excerpted from the following *JAMA*-copyrighted article: Rasekh Z, Bauer H, Manos M, Iacopino V. Women's Health and Human Rights in Afghanistan. *JAMA*. 1998; 280(5):449-455.

[124] A cross-sectional survey of demographics, health status, war-related trauma, and human rights experiences and attitudes was conducted by interview. Marked restriction on women's movements, prohibition on interacting with expatriates, and the risk of summary punishment for acts which authorities consider threatening precluded random sampling of the general population in Kabul. For this reason, both probability and non-probability samples of women living in Kabul and women who migrated from Kabul to Pakistan were used.

[125] Patton MQ. *Qualitative Evaluation and Research Methods*. Newbury Park, CA: Sage Publications; 1990:169-283.

Afghan women living in Peshawar or Islamabad were identified through chain sampling with the initial cases being referred by several humanitarian assistance organizations. In Pakistan, every woman we approached (80/80) agreed to participate and completed the interview.

Survey Questionnaire

The survey contained 101 questions focusing on physical and mental health status, access to health care, landmine injuries and awareness education, war-related experiences, human rights abuses, and attitudes towards women's human rights. Questions regarding human rights abuses and attitudes towards women's human rights appeared last to allow time to establish rapport and assess the safety of completing the interview.

Post-traumatic stress disorder (PTSD) was assessed by a trained health professional using the 17 *Diagnostic and Statistical Manual of Mental Disorders-IV* (DSM-IV)[126] symptoms for PTSD scored on a four-point severity scale. Symptom scores greater than 2.5 were considered significant. The clinical diagnosis of PTSD was defined according to established criteria, at least one of the four intrusive symptoms, three of the seven avoidance symptoms, and two of the six increased arousal symptoms for at least three months over the past year.[127]

The Hopkins Symptom Checklist-25 (HSCL-25)[128] was used to assess symptoms of depression and anxiety "within the past week." Mean cumulative scores above 1.75 were used to predict the clinical diagnosis of major depression[129] and to identify significant symptoms of anxiety.[130]

Health status and access to and quality of health care were assessed using Likert-type scales (e.g. excellent, good, fair, poor). In addition, physical and mental health condition during the past two years were assessed using severity scales of 0 to 20. Decline in physical or mental condition was calculated using self-reported ratings for "the past year" and "two years ago."

The questionnaire was written in English and then translated into Farsi (a widely spoken, official language in Afghanistan). Five regional

---

[126] American Psychiatric Association. *Diagnostic and Statistical Manual of Mental Disorders, Fourth Edition*. Washington (DC). American Psychiatric Association; 1994.

[127] *Id.*

[128] Mollica RF, Wyshak G, de Marneffe D, et al. Indochinese versions of the Hopkins Symptom Checklist-25, a screening instrument for the psychiatric care of refugees. *Am J Psychiatry*. 1987; 144:497-500.

[129] *Id.* and Hinton WL, Du N, Chen YC, Tran CH, Newman TB, Lu FG. Screening for major depression in Vietnamese refugees: a validation and comparative of two instruments in a health screening population. *J Gen Intern Med*. 1994; 9(4):202-6.

[130] Mollica RF et al, *Supra*, 128

experts in health and human rights reviewed the questionnaire for content validity. The survey was pilot tested among eight Afghan women in Pakistan and suggestions were incorporated for clarity of questions and cultural appropriateness.

Interviews

All interviews were conducted during a three-month study period in early 1998 by a PHR health researcher in Farsi. Each interview was conducted in the most private setting possible and lasted approximately two hours. Verbal informed consent was obtained and participants did not receive any material recompense. Participant's names and addresses were not recorded for security purposes.

Ethnicity was determined indirectly, because the vast majority of the Taliban are from the Pashtun ethnic group, and many Afghans are sensitive to questions of ethnicity. The respondent's ethnicity was scored as Pashtun only if the respondent spoke Pashto and/or voluntarily disclosed the information.

Statistical Analysis

The data were analyzed using SPSS statistical software.[131] For 2x2 cross tabulations containing cells with expected frequencies of less than 5, statistical significance was determined using Fisher's exact test; Yates' corrected chi square was used for all others. For cross tabulations with greater than two rows, statistical significance was determined using Pearson chi square. Analysis of variance (ANOVA) was used for statistical comparison of means and the Kruskal-Wallis test was used for comparison of medians. For all statistical determinations, significance levels were established at $p < 0.05$.

Definitions

Family members were defined as either immediate members (husband, children, parents, and siblings) or extended members (aunts, uncles, nieces, nephews, and cousins). Daily activities that may have been affected by one's physical and/or mental condition included: caring for children, cooking, cleaning, going to the market, social activities and work, if employed. Torture, in this study, was defined according to the UN Convention Against Torture[132] and public beatings were considered single episodes of beating of limited duration (less than 10 minutes) and intensity.

---

[131] *SPSS Base 7.5 for Windows.* 1997. SPSS Inc., Chicago IL.

[132] *Twenty-five Human Rights Documents.* Columbia University Press: New York, NY: Convention Against Torture and Other Cruel, Inhuman, or Degrading Treatment or Punishment. 1994.

Study Limitations

Limitations in sampling preclude the results of this study from being generalizable to all women in Afghanistan. Also, the study was designed to describe the health and human rights status of Afghan women, not to compare differences among specific sample groups or to test hypotheses. Therefore, attribution of health and human rights outcomes to specific factors is limited. The use of random sampling of lists from humanitarian assistance organizations, and chain sampling with initial cases referred by these organizations, may have over-represented women in need of humanitarian assistance.

Characteristics of Afghan Women Respondents

Demographic characteristics of the study respondents are presented in Table 1. The median age for respondents was 32 years (range 17-70) years. The majority (81 or 51%) of respondents were married. Of the women living in Pakistan, more were married than were not, whereas more women living in Kabul were single. Pashtun ethnicity was represented in 14% (23) of the sample. The majority (85%) of respondents lived in Kabul during the past 19 years of civil unrest and armed conflict. Also noteworthy is that 74 women living in Pakistan (93%) had lived in Kabul 19 or more years. Sixty-eight of the 80 participants (85%) living in Pakistan had migrated after the Taliban suspended medical services to women in Kabul in September, 1997.

The median level of respondents' formal education was 12 years. Although 99 (62%) of the respondents reported a variety of occupations and were employed when the Taliban took control of Kabul, only 32 (20%) were employed during their last year in Kabul. Unemployment rates were higher among women living in Pakistan (67 or 84%) compared to women living in Kabul (61 or 76%). The median household monthly income during their last year in Kabul was $6 (US dollars) and was higher among women living in Kabul. Consistent with these income data, women in Pakistan reported more crowded living conditions at the time of the study. In spite of these economic hardships, only 10 women (6%) reported receiving any form of humanitarian assistance while living in Kabul.

Table 1.
**Respondent Characteristics for Afghan Women's
Health and Human Rights Survey***

Respondent Characteristics	Afghan women living in Kabul (n=80)	Afghan women living in Pakistan (n=80)	Total (N=160)
Age in years (median, range)	31 (17-55)	33 (20-70)	32 (17-70)
Marital status No. (%)			
Single	21 (26)	5 (6)†	26 (16)
Married	34 (43)	47 (59)	81 (51)
Divorced	3 (4)	2 (3)	5 (3)
Widowed	22 (28)	26 (33)	48 (30)
Ethnic group No. (%)			
Pashtun	9 (11)	14 (18)	23 (14)
Non-Pashtun	71 (89)	66 (83)	137 (86)
Lived in Kabul 19 or more years No. (%)	62 (78)	74 (93)†	136 (85)
Years of education (median, range)	13.5 (0-19)	12 (0-19)†	12 (0-19)
Occupation in Kabul No. (%)			
Housewife/student	32 (40)	29 (36)	61 (38)
Clerk/nurse/health technician/other	16 (20)	23 (29)	39 (24)
Professional/educator	32 (40)	28 (35)	60 (38)
Employment status in Kabul No. (%)			
Working (part or full-time)	19 (24)	13 (16)†	32 (20)
Unemployed (officially prohibited)	45 (56)	45 (56)	90 (56)
Unemployed (other reasons)	16 (20)	22 (28)	38 (24)
Household monthly income in Kabul, US $ (median, range)	14 (0-517)	4 (0-86)†	6 (0-517)
Household members per room currently (median, range)	3.0 (0.3-8)	6.0 (0.3-15)†	4.5 (0.3-15)
Received humanitarian assistance in Kabul No. (%)	7 (9)	3 (4)	10 (6)

*Values are number (percent) unless otherwise indicated.
†P<.05.

Physical Health and Access to Health Care

The respondents' self-reported physical health status and access to medical treatment are described in Table 2. In general, Afghan women living in Pakistan reported worse health status and poorer access to health care than women remaining in Kabul during the last two years. Eighty-three (52%) or respondents described their physical health as fair or poor. Overall, 113 respondents (71%) reported a decline in their health (at least five points on a 0-20 scale) during the past year in Kabul compared with two years prior.

Overall, 59 (37%) of respondents reported that their health conditions significantly interfered with daily activities. Afghan women reported a variety of medical problems. The most commonly reported medical conditions included chronic musculoskeletal pain (78 or 49%), gastrointestinal symptoms (51 or 32%), gynecological symptoms (36 or 23%), and chronic headaches (30 or 19%). In addition, 37 (28%) of 131 applicable respondents reported having "very little" or "no control" on the timing and spacing of their births.

The majority of respondents (122 or 77%) reported poor access to health care services in Kabul during the past year of residence there; an additional 31 (20%) reported no access. Both the access to care and the quality of health care services in Kabul were deemed "much worse" during the past year compared with two years prior by a majority of the participants (99 or 62% and 92 or 58%, respectively). Eighty-five women (53%) described occasions in which they were quite ill and unable to seek medical care. Of those, 47 (55%) said they lacked access, 29 (34%) cited economic barriers, and 9 (11%) said curfews restricted their movement in public. Reasons cited for being unable to seek care included lack of access (55%), economic barriers (34%), and curfews restricting their movement in public (11%). In addition, 150 (94%) of study participants believed that the health of women in Afghanistan would be improved by increasing access to health care services (including mental health and rehabilitation services), increasing humanitarian assistance, improving access to reproductive health services (including family planning), and allowing women to control the timing and spacing of their children.

Table 2.
Health Status and Access and Quality of Care of Afghan Women Living in Kabul, Afghanistan and in Refugee Settings in Pakistan

Health Status	Afghan women living in Kabul (n=80)	Afghan women living in Pakistan (n=80)	Total (N=160)
Reported "fair" or "poor" general health condition over the past year No. (%)	31 (39)	52 (65)*	83 (52)
Decline in physical condition over the past 2 years of ≥ 5 on a 0-20 scale No. (%)	43 (54)	70 (89)*	113 (71)
Reported physical condition interfered with daily activities "quite a bit" or "almost totally" No. (%)	17 (21)	42 (53)*	59 (37)
Reported "very little" or "no control" over the timing and spacing of births No. (% of applicable cases)	22/56 (39)	15/75 (20)*	37/131 (28)

Access and Quality of Health Care†	Afghan women living in Kabul (n=80)	Afghan women living in Pakistan (n=80)	Total (N=160)
Reported access to health care No. (%)			
No access	1 (1)	30 (38)*	31 (20)
Poor access	73 (92)	49 (61)	122 (77)
Adequate or good access	5 (6)	1 (1)	6 (4)
Reported access to health care services "much worse" No. (%)	37 (47)	62 (78)*	99 (62)
Reported health services to be "much worse" No. (%)	34 (43)	58 (73)*	92 (58)
Reported being seriously ill and unable to seek care No. (%)	40 (50)	45 (56)	85 (53)

*P<.05.

†During the last 2 years of residence in Kabul.

Mental Health Status

The participants reported declining mental health and had symptoms of psychiatric disorders (Table 3). Overall, 129 (81%) of respondents reported a decline in their mental health (at least five points on a 0-20 scale) during the past year in Kabul compared with two years prior; 56 (35%) of respondents reported that their mental conditions significantly interfered with daily activities. Based on self-reported symptoms, 67 (42%) respondents met the diagnostic criteria for PTSD; 155 (97%) met the criteria for major depression, and 137 (86%) demonstrated significant symptoms of anxiety. One hundred and fifty-one (94%) reported significant intrusive symptoms, and 152 (95%) reported increased arousal symptoms of PTSD. In general, Afghan women living in Pakistan reported worse mental health status and demonstrated higher percentages of PTSD, major depression and significant anxiety symptoms than did women remaining in Kabul. Overall, 158 (98%) of respondents met criteria for either PTSD, major depression, or significant symptoms of anxiety, 83 (52%) met criteria for two of these, and 59 (37%) met criteria for all three.

Table 3.
Mental Health Status and Psychological
Diagnoses and Significant Symptoms*

Mental Health Status	Afghan women living in Kabul (n=80)	Afghan women living in Pakistan (n=80)	Total (N=160)
Decline in mental condition over the past two years of ≥ 5 on a 0-20 scale No. (%)	56 (70)	73 (91)†	129 (81)
Reported mental condition interfered with daily activities "quite a bit" or "almost totally" No.(%)	14 (18)	42 (53)†	56 (35)
Psychological Diagnoses and Significant Symptoms			
PTSD diagnosis (DSM-IV Criteria) No. (%)	41 (51)	26 (33)†	67 (42)
Significant intrusive symptoms	72 (90)	79 (99)†	151 (94)
Significant avoidance symptoms	44 (55)	26 (33)†	70 (44)
Significant increased arousal symptoms	74 (93)	78 (98)	152 (95)
Depression diagnosis No. (%)	75 (94)	80 (100)†	155 (97)
Significant anxiety symptoms No. (%)	67 (84)	70 (88)	137 (86)

*PTSD indicates post-traumatic stress disorder; DSM-IV, Diagnostic and Statistical
Manual of Mental Disorders, Fourth Edition.
†$P<.05$.

War-Related Experiences and Landmine Exposures

The respondents reported notable war-related losses and hardships (Table
4). Most of the study participants, 134 (84%), reported that one or more
family members had been killed in the war; 112 (70%) reported war-related injuries among their family members. The median number of displacements from Kabul because of the war was 1 (range 0-3). Only one
participant reported never having been displaced. More than 128 (80%) of
all respondents were displaced one or more times within Kabul between
1992 and September, 1996. The most commonly cited hardships during
displacement included poverty, disease, emotional difficulties, lack of access to health care services, lack of access to education, and inadequate
sanitation. Afghan women living in Pakistan consistently reported higher
percentages of displacement hardships than did women living in Kabul.

Overall, 25 (16%) of respondents reported that one or more family
members were killed by landmines, and 36 (23%) reported injuries to
family members caused by landmines. Despite the high rates of injury
and death, only 76 (48%) of respondents had received landmine awareness education or training. Among 113 women with children, 70 (62%)

reported that their children had received landmine awareness education or training. One hundred fifty study participants (94%) believed that the health of women in Afghanistan would be improved by improving landmine awareness education and clearance of landmines.

Table 4.
War-Related Experiences and Landmine Issues*

War-Related Experiences	Afghan women living in Kabul (n=80)	Afghan women living in Pakistan (n=80)	Total (N=160)
Reported one or more family members killed in war No. (%)			
Immediate family members	43 (54)	29 (36)	72 (45)
Extended family members	27 (34)	35 (44)	62 (39)
Reported one or more family members injured in war No. (%)			
Immediate family members	22 (28)	32 (40)†	54 (34)
Extended family members	27 (34)	31 (39)	58 (36)
Times displaced from Kabul city (median range)	2.0 (0-3)	1.0 (1-3)†	1.0 (0-3)
Reported one or more displacements No. (%)	79 (99)	80 (100)	159 (99)
Displacement hardships‡			
Economic hardship	36 (45)	74 (93)†	110 (69)
Serious illness	43 (54)	65 (81)†	108 (68)
Emotional disturbances	34 (43)	67 (84)†	101 (63)
No access to health care	28 (35)	58 (73)†	86 (54)
No access to education	29 (36)	52 (65)†	81 (51)
Inadequate sanitation	21 (26)	59 (74)†	80 (50)
Landmine Injury and Education			
Reported one or more family members killed by landmines No. (%)	11 (14)	14 (18)	25 (16)
Reported one or more family members injured by landmines No. (%)	19 (24)	17 (21)	36 (23)
Reported landmine awareness education No. (%)	40 (50)	36 (45)	76 (48)
Reported landmine awareness education for children □	36/45 (80)	34/68 (50)†	70/113 (62)

*Values are number (percent) unless otherwise indicated.
†P<.05.
‡Number and percent represent those who have been displaced.
□ Number and percent represent those with children (n=113).

Human Rights Violations

The respondents reported harassment, physical abuse, and restricted activity as a consequence of the Taliban occupation in Kabul (Table 5). One hundred eleven (69%) of participants reported that they or a family member had been detained in Kabul by Taliban religious police or security forces. Overall, 35 respondents (22%) reported a total of 43 separate incidents in which they were detained and abused. Of these incidents, 31 (72%) followed non-adherence to the Taliban's dress code for women. Specific offenses included: not wearing a *burqa*; not completely covering the face, hands, wrists or feet; and wearing stylish clothes, and wearing white socks or white shoes or shoes that make noise when walking. Five (12%) respondents were detained for being unaccompanied by a male chaperone in public. Among other detainees, two disabled women, both of whom lost a leg from rocket blast injuries, were detained and beaten for entering a public building through a designated male entrance. The majority (35 (81%) of 43) of detentions lasted less than 1 hour; however, 36 (84%) resulted in public beatings and one (2%) in torture.

Ninety-two study participants (58%) reported that a family member had been detained in a total of 133 separate incidents. Of the 17 incidents involving female family members, the reasons for detention and abuse were similar to those identified by the respondents. Of the 116 incidents involving male family members, reasons for detention included having a short beard (29 or 25%) and being a member of a minority ethnic group (mainly Tajik and Hazara) (32 or 28%). Other reasons for detention of men included not being in a mosque at prayer time, flying a kite, playing music at their wedding, and laughing in public. The majority (70 (60%) of 116) of these detentions lasted longer than one hour; 63 (54%) resulted in beatings and 24 (21%) resulted in torture.

Sixty-two (39%) percent of respondents reported that they were "extremely concerned" about being detained and abused by Taliban religious police when leaving their home and an additional 65 (41%) reported being "quite a bit concerned" about their safety. One hundred eight participants (68%) reported that they had "extremely restricted" their activities in public during the past year in Kabul. Only 3 respondents (2%) reported "no restriction" on their activities. Women living in Pakistan reported higher percentages of human rights abuses, extremely restricted activities, and extreme concern for their safety in public. Consistent with these differences, 62 Afghan women living in Pakistan (78%) cited their own security and that of their families, 71 (89%) cited economic hardship, and 49 (61%) cited restrictions on women's human rights as reasons for leaving Kabul.

Table 5.
Human Rights Abuses Reported by Respondents

Human Rights Abuses	Afghan women living in Kabul (n=80)	Afghan women living in Pakistan (n=80)	Total (N=160)
Self or family member detained/abused in Kabul over the past two years No. (%)	46 (58)	65 (81)*	111 (69)
Respondents detained/abused No. (%)	12 (15)	23 (29)*	35 (22)
Number of incidents	12	31	43
Family member detained/abused No. (%)	34 (43)	58 (73)*	92 (58)
Number of incidents	49	84	133
Reported "extreme" fear when in public in Kabul over the past two years No. (%)	18 (23)	44 (55)*	62 (39)
Reported restricted public/social activities "extremely" in Kabul over the past two years No. (%)	41 (51)	67 (84)*	108 (68)

*P<.05.

Attitudes Toward Women's Human Rights

Nearly all study participants were in agreement on the issues of women's human rights listed in Table 6. More than 95% of respondents agreed that women should have equal access to education, equal work opportunities, freedom of expression, freedom of association, freedom of movement, control over the number and spacing of children, legal protection for women's human rights, and participation in government. More than 95% disagreed with Taliban dress codes and believed that the teachings of Islam do not inherently impose restrictions on women's human rights. In assessing future recommendations, 150 (94%) of study participants believed that the health of women in Afghanistan would be improved by involving women in the United Nations peace process in Afghanistan, ending armed conflict in Afghanistan, and changing the political control in the country.

Table 6.
Majority Opinions* on Women's Human Rights

- Strict dress codes for women are not appropriate.
- Women should have equal access to education.
- Women should have equal work opportunities.
- Women should be able to express themselves freely.
- Women should be able to associate with people of their choosing.
- Women should be able to move about in society without restriction.
- Women should be able to control the number and spacing of their children.
- There should be legal protections for the rights of women.
- Women should be able to participate in government.
- The teachings of Islam do not inherently restrict women's human rights.

*Opinions shared by more than 95% of all respondents.

Comments on Survey Findings

Human rights are founded on principles that all members of the human family are equal in dignity and rights.[133] However, where discrimination against women exists, women are often excluded from effective participation in identifying and securing their rights. In Afghanistan, Taliban restrictions on women's participation in society make it nearly impossible for women to represent their health and human rights interests.

This study was designed to survey women who would otherwise not have the opportunity for effective representation, to enable them to identify the health and human rights problems they have experienced in recent years under Taliban rule, and to convey their attitudes regarding women's human rights. PHR's purpose was to understand better the nature and extent of human right abuses in Afghanistan and the impact on women's physical and mental health.

In general, respondents represented a wide age range, diverse educational and occupational backgrounds, and all levels of income. At the time of this survey the majority were unemployed, poor, and living in crowded conditions. The Pashtun ethnicity, which is often associated with the Taliban faction, was represented. In striking contrast to published reports indicating the successful disbursement of humanitarian assistance,[134] only 10 respondents (6%) reported receiving any form of

---

[133] See *Twenty-five Human Rights Documents*. Center for the Study of Human Rights. Columbia University Press: New York, NY: Excerpts from the Charter of the United Nations. 1994; and *Twenty-five Human Rights Documents*. Center for the Study of Human Rights. Columbia University Press: New York, NY: Universal Declaration of Human Rights. 1994.

[134] *E/CN.4/1996/64, Supra,29.*

humanitarian assistance while living in Kabul. One explanation may be that Taliban gender restrictions interfere with the delivery of humanitarian assistance to women.[135]

In comparison to the Kabul samples, the Afghan women who migrated to Pakistan were more likely to be married, reported fewer years of education and had smaller household incomes than in Kabul. Perhaps these factors influenced their motivation to flee their country. Their report of high levels of crowded living conditions in Pakistan may attest to their sacrifices.

Since the beginning of the Taliban occupation, the majority of respondents reported that their health and physical conditions had declined significantly. Also, Afghan women reported inadequate control over their reproduction. After having experienced years of armed conflict and injuries to themselves or their families,[136] they are now forbidden from working and receiving formal education, restricted in their activities in public, and are targets of attack by Taliban militia.[137] These oppressive violations of women's human rights likely have a detrimental influence on health, particularly in the types of stress-related symptoms reported here.

The majority of respondents reported that their access to and quality of health care were inadequate. These findings are in accordance with previous reports that found only 26% of the total population were receiving treatment for common diseases and injuries.[138] Taliban restrictions that preclude women from receiving adequate medical care[139] are likely to have contributed to the respondents' decline in access to care. Our finding that Afghan women living in Pakistan were more likely to report poorer health and poorer access may indicate that many of these women lived in Kabul when medical services were suspended for women and migrated to refugee camps or cities in Pakistan before the Taliban eased restrictions to non-segregated hospitals in November 1997.

Based on self-reported symptoms, there was a high prevalence of poor mental health among study participants, both subjectively and diagnostically based on self-reported symptoms. The frequency of symptoms of

---

[135] *Country Report on Human Rights, Supra*, 3.

[136] *Id.*; See also *E/CN.4/1996/64, Supra*, 29 at 119; and United Nations High Commissioner for Refugees. Focus: Afghanistan the Unending Crises. *Refugees*. 1997;108:3-9.

[137] *E/CN.4/1996/64, Supra, 29 at* 119.

[138] *DHA Report, Supra, 1.*

[139] See *Country Report on Human Rights, Supra* 3 at, 120; and Block M. Kabul's health apartheid, *Supra*, 3.

PTSD, major depression, and anxiety among the study participants exceeded that found in refugee populations receiving mental health services in the United States.[140] Although the prevalence of major depression and significant symptoms of anxiety among study participants was high, other studies have demonstrated similar findings. One study observed major depression in 80% of a random sample of Cambodian refugees living in the United States.[141] That Afghan women continue to experience considerable traumas and hardships may account for the higher percentages of depression (or significant anxiety symptoms) observed in this study. Inasmuch as previous research has demonstrated that there are strong correlations between war trauma and high rates of PTSD and affective disorder, we believe that the war and the Taliban occupation almost certainly have profoundly affected these women's mental health.[142] The low frequency of avoidance symptoms reported by all participants may be due to the presence of ongoing traumatic experiences.

The Afghan women in our study reported high prevalences of family members being lost to war and displacement hardships. The majority of study participants were long-term residents of Kabul and were likely affected by the violence and abuses that occurred during the Soviet occupation and followed by subsequent factional armed conflicts. The increased numbers of displacements and greater reporting of hardships among women who migrated to Pakistan may reflect a selection factor for migration.

Many study participants reported injury and death within their family from landmines. It is estimated that since 1992 landmines have killed more than 20,000 people and injured more than 400,000 others in

---

[140] See Kinzie JD, Boehnlein JK, Leung PK, Moore LJ, Riley C, Smith D. The prevalence of post-traumatic stress disorder and its clinical significance among Southeast Asian refugees. *Am. J. Psychiatry*. 1990; 147:913-7; Mollica RF, *Supra* 129; Westermeyer J, Vang TF, Neider J. A comparison of refugees using and not using psychiatric service: an analysis of DSM-III criteria and self-rated scales in cross-cultural context. *J. Operational Psychiatry*. 1983; 14:36-41; and Mghir R, Freed W, Raskin A, Katon W. Depression and post-traumatic stress disorder among a community sample of adolescent and young adult Afghan refugees. *J. Nerv. Ment. Dis*. 1995; 183:24-30.

[141] Carlson EB, Rosser-Hogan R. Trauma experiences, post-traumatic stress, dissociation and depression in Cambodian refugees. *Am. J. Psychiatry*. 1991; 148(11):1548-51.

[142] See Kinzie JD, Boehnlein JK, Leung PK, Moore LJ, Riley C Smith D. The prevalence of post-traumatic stress disorder and its clinical significance among Southeast Asian refugees. *Am. J. Psychiatry*. 1990; 147:913-7; Mollica RF, *Supra*, 129; Westermeyer J, Vang TF, Neider J. A comparison of refugees using and not using psychiatric service: an analysis of DSM-III criteria and self-rated scales in cross-cultural context. *J. Operational Psychiatry*. 1983; 14:36-41; and Mghir R, Freed W, Raskin A, Katon W. Depression and post-traumatic stress disorder among a community sample of adolescent and young adult Afghan refugees. *J. Nerv Ment Dis*. 1995; 183:24-30.

Women from all walks of life are forced to conceal themselves in public with a shroud-like *burqa*, or else face beatings. These women were waiting to be examined in a women's clinic. Those without a *burqa* have no such opportunity for health care.

Household items for sale by a family in Kabul in order to survive.

A 35-year-old former teacher with her children. She was able to feed the children only by donning her *burqa* and begging in the streets of Kabul every day.

A portion of an unexploded ordinance (UXO) protruding from a house in a residential area of western Kabul.

An alleged murderer, surrounded by Taliban armed men, kneels on the ground of the Kabul sports stadium a few minutes before his execution. Thousands of Kabul residents were summoned to witness this execution, as they are every Friday for other executions, amputations and other punishments.

Not permitted to enter NGO buildings and talk to foreign aid workers, Afghan women wait outside for hours hoping to obtain humanitarian assistance.

"First, I lost my husband, then the Taliban took my job; now, like a professional beggar I have my own spot on the side of the road," said a young widow. For many women, begging has become the only means of survival under the Taliban's restrictions for women.

A young girl, pushing her paraplegic and blind father on the streets of Kabul, begs for money. The father lost his legs and vision in a landmine accident a few years ago. Her mother could not work due to Taliban policies.

A 12-year-old boy, working as a shopkeeper's assistant and supporting his three younger siblings and parents, started to cry when he expressed his concerns about the rising costs of wheat flour, oil, and other cooking essentials. He was also traumatized after having attended a public execution in the Kabul sports stadium.

A 42-year-old former teacher, living with her children in a refugee camp in Pakistan, lost her right leg when a rocket hit her home in Kabul. The rocket killed her husband. She was beaten twice by Taliban officials: once for entering city hall through the "male-only" entrance, the other for boarding a public bus through a back door.

Children playing in a destroyed residential area contaminated with mines and UXOs (unexploded ordnances).

An operating room in one of the few female health facilities in Kabul. There was no running water, sterile gloves or sterilization equipment.

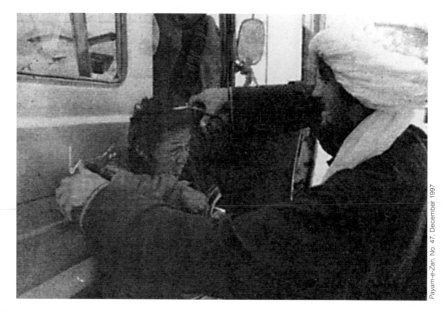

Payam-e-Zan, No. 47, December 1997

A member of the Taliban religious police forcibly cutting the hair of a man accused of having a "Western" hairstyle.

Ascanio Raffaelle Circello

Afghan women, in modest clothing, on the streets of Kabul a few months prior to Taliban takeover. Before the Taliban, women played a prominent role in the health professions, in government, and in teaching.

Afghanistan.[143] Approximately 80% of the landmine casualties are civilian and among these 40-50% are women and children.[144] In spite of this imminent danger and the relatively high rates of loss and injury to landmines, the study participants reported inadequate awareness education.

Many women in our study reported being detained by Taliban religious police and security forces for violating the dress code and that commonly such detentions resulted in public beatings. Many of the participants also described incidents in which male family members were subjected to beatings and torture for violating male dress and hair length codes. According to Taliban edicts, men's beards must protrude farther than would a fist clamped at the base of the chin; men who do not comply are subjected to public beatings, torture, and imprisonment.[145] Under these circumstances, many participants reported being extremely concerned for their safety and being severely restricted in their public activities. The reasons for detention and abuse of respondents and their family members provide some insight into the nature of Taliban repression and the means by which it is enforced.

Afghan women living in Pakistan reported the greatest number of incidents (per person) in which they were detained and had a higher percent of safety concerns and restrictions regarding their activities in public. There is some evidence that these experiences influenced their decision to leave Kabul in that safety concerns and women's rights restrictions were commonly cited as reasons for leaving Kabul. Alternatively, women living in Kabul may have reported fewer cases of abuse if they feared retaliation by the Taliban forces.

Nearly all of the women surveyed supported women's human rights. Given their support for women's human rights in this study, it appears that Taliban policies regarding the role of women in society do not represent the interests of the individuals they claim to serve. Taliban repression combines restrictions regarding minute details of its residents' personal lives justified in the name of their interpretation of Islamic law,[146] with violent and often arbitrary enforcement.[147]

---

[143] US Committee for Refugees. *World Refugee Survey*, 1997. Washington, DC: US Committee for Refugees; 1997:124-125.

[144] *Country Report on Human Rights, Supra, 3* at 120.

[145] *Id.*

[146] *E/CN.4/1996/64, Supra,*29 at 119. Also see World Health Organization. Hope. World Health Organization. December, 1996; and E/CN.4/1997/59, *Supra*, 22.

[147] *E/CN.4/1997/59, Supra,*22.

IV. INTERVIEWS WITH AFGHAN WOMEN AND HEALTH EXPERTS

Methods

In order to put the findings of PHR's health and human rights survey in context and to hear how those who are subject to repression experience it — and how it affects their physical and mental health — PHR gathered testimony regarding individual experiences through semi-structured interviews of 40 Afghan women. Twenty of the women interviewed lived in Kabul, while the other 20 were residing in Pakistan, having fled from Kabul. All of the women who fled to Pakistan did so after the Taliban took control of Kabul. The women were identified primarily through "snowball or chain" sampling. Others had been randomly selected to participate in the interviews, but were not available at the time the interviews were conducted. In a few cases, women who saw an interview in process (for example, at a health clinic) volunteered to speak to the interviewer and thus were included as a case as well. One interviewer collected all 40 of the case testimonies.

The semi-structured interview was based upon 26 questions. The discussion focused on five primary areas: the general living conditions in Kabul; health status and access to care; war-related trauma, including landmine experience; human rights abuses; and women's human rights experiences and attitudes. The average interview lasted 45 to 60 minutes. Most of the Kabul interviews were conducted in the women's homes or in a hospital or NGO health clinic. In Pakistan, the testimonies were obtained either in women's homes, refugee camps, or in health clinics. Only one interview had to be stopped. In Pakistan, a woman's husband returned home while the interview was in process. He expressed concern to his wife regarding their safety should she continue, and thus she asked that it be stopped. A second interview was not fully completed due to time constraints. Consequently, the completed portions of these two cases are included among the narrative case summaries. These cases did not have sufficient information to include them in the summary of case findings in Table 7.

In the vast majority of cases, the women were enthusiastic, although somewhat fearful, about speaking out on their living conditions. During the interviews, about two-thirds of the women cried openly as they described their situations. They typically became very upset during the interview, and expressed considerable anger and outrage over the Taliban policies regarding women. Some of the anger was projected on the interviewer; many women felt that the international community was not responding to their plight as women. However, many were hopeful that something productive would result from PHR's effort. It was this reason that many of the women risked talking, for most had fears about their names and opinions falling into the Taliban's hands.

To protect the anonymity of the women, PHR is not releasing any of the respondents' names or identifying characteristics. All forty women who participated in the case histories are referred to by non-identifying case report numbers. Women from Kabul are referred to as K1 through K20. Women from Pakistan are referred to as P1 to P20.

To provide another perspective on the treatment of women in Afghanistan today, PHR also interviewed twelve health experts workers about the problems Afghan women face and their own experiences providing assistance to Afghan women. Because of PHR's particular concern with women's health status, ten of those interviewed were trained health professionals (seven physicians and three nurses) working for organizations promoting health programs in Afghanistan. In addition, we interviewed two journalists with expertise in health and development issues. Because of the concern about possible governmental reprisals against them and their organizations, PHR guaranteed that their identities would remain confidential. Interviews were based on a set of open-ended questions, with all answers recorded on the sheet of questions. These are identified as H1 to H12.

This section includes testimonies of the women interviewed along with the observations of PHR's researcher and secondary sources. It covers four types of human rights violations women in Afghanistan face — access to health care, employment, education, and mobility — then explores the impact of these violations on their lives.

Summary of Semi-Structured Interviews with Afghan Women

Transcripts of interviews with the 40 Afghan women were reviewed and descriptive information was recorded for 38 of the cases as presented in Table 7.[148] The high degree of correlation between the findings of PHR's health and human rights survey and the semi-structured interviews is further evidence of the generalizability of the findings of this study.

---

[148] Two of the interviews were not fully completed and therefore not included in the summary of findings in Table 7.

Demographic characteristics of those interviewed were similar to those observed in PHR's health and human rights survey (see Chapter III). The mean age of the women interviewed was 31 (range, 18 to 57) years. Many of the women had professional occupations in Kabul (42%) or were clerks, nurses, health technicians, etc. (24%), however, only 13% were employed.[149]

The women who PHR interviewed described declining physical health and access to health care in the past two years similar to that observed in the health and human rights survey. Among the 38 women with completed interviews, 66% indicated a decline in physical condition and 87% described decreased access to health services in Kabul during the past two years. Of the 33 women who indicated decreased access to health services, reasons included the following: economic (61%), no female doctor, (48%), restrictions on women's movement (36%), no chaperone available (27%), hospital refused to treat them, (21%), or do not own a *burqa*, (6%). In addition, 95% (36 of 38 women interviewed) described a decline in their mental condition.

The vast majority of women interviewed described war-related trauma and hardships. Seventy-nine percent (30 of 38 women interviewed) reported one or more family member killed in the war, which is similar to the rate of 84% reported in PHR's health and human rights survey. Twenty-six percent (10 of 38 women interviewed) reported one or more family member injured in the war. In addition, seventy-six percent (29 of 38 women interviewed) indicated that they had been displaced from Kabul one or more times. The most common displacement hardships that they experienced were: emotional disturbances (93%), economic hardship (86%), no access to education (79%), no or poor access to health care (76%), and serious illness (34%). Of the 38 women interviewed, 2 (5%) reported one or more family member killed by landmines. Only 29% of women (11 of 38 women interviewed) reported receiving landmine awareness education. Among the 21 women who had children, 12 (57%) received landmine awareness education.

The physical abuse that women reported was strikingly similar to that observed in PHR's health and human rights survey. Sixty-eight percent (26 of 38 women interviewed) described incidents in which they were detained and physically abused by Taliban officials.[150] Of the 7 women who were detained and abused by Taliban officials, 86% followed non-adherence to dress codes and 14% were detained and abused for not being ac-

---

[149] The relatively high proportion of professionals among those interviewed is most likely due to the fact that the initial cases referred in the chain sample were health professionals.

[150] In PHR's health and human rights survey, 69% of respondents reported that they or a family member had been detained and physically abused by Taliban officials. See Chapter III.

companied by a chaperone. Of the 19 family members who were detained and abused, 32% were related to violations of beard or hair codes; 32% were based on ethnicity, and 36% were for a variety of other reasons. Of the 26 women who described incidents of detention and abuse by Taliban officials, the types of abuse reported included: beating (50%), incarceration (23%), torture (12%), among others (15%).

Taliban restrictions on education, employment and freedom of movement have had profound effects on women. All of the women interviewed (38) reported lack of access to education in the past two years and 74% (28 of 38 women interviewed) indicated that they had become unemployed due to Taliban policies. In addition, 81% of women reported restricting their public and social activities in Kabul over the past two years because of Taliban policies.

Ninety-seven percent (37 of 38 interviewed) reported that women's human rights had deteriorated markedly over the past two years. Also, ninety-seven percent (37 of 38 interviewed) indicated that they believed the teachings of Islam do not inherently impose restrictions on women's human rights.

Table 7.
Summary Findings of Interviews with Forty Afghan Women[151]

Characteristic	Response Number	(%)
Occupation		
Housewife/student	13	(34)
Clerk/nurse/health technician/other	9	(24)
Professional/educator	16	(42)
Residence		
Kabul	20	(50)
Pakistan camp	5	(13)
Pakistan city	13	(38)
Employment status in Kabul No. (%)		
Working (part or full-time)	5	(13)
Unemployed	33	(87)
Officially prohibited (n=33)	27	(82)
Other reasons (n=33)	6	(18)
Health Status and Access to Care		
Decline in physical condition over the past 2 years	25	(66)
Decreased access to health services in Kabul x 2 years	33	(87)
Reasons: Economic (n=33)	20	(61)
No female doctor (n=33)	16	(48)

[151] Values are number (percent) unless otherwise indicated.

Characteristic	Response Number	(%)
Restrictions on women's movement (n=33)	12	(36)
No chaperone available (n=33)	9	(27)
Hospital refused (n=33)	7	(21)
Do not own a *burqa* (n=33)	2	(6)
Decline in mental condition over the past two years	36	(95)
War-Related Trauma and Landmine Issues		
Reported one or more family members killed in war	30	(79)
Immediate family members (n=30)	17	(57)
Extended family members (n=30)	13	(43)
Reported one or more family members injured in war	10	(26)
Immediate family members (n=10)	5	(50)
Extended family members (n=10)	5	(50)
Reported one or more displacements No. (%)	29	(76)
Displacement hardships		
Emotional disturbances (n=29)	27	(93)
Economic hardship (n=29)	25	(86)
No access to education (n=29)	23	(79)
No or poor access to health care (n=29)	22	(76)
Serious illness (n=29)	10	(34)
Reported one or more family members killed by landmines	2	(5)
Reported one or more family members injured by landmines	0	(0)
Reported landmine awareness education	11	(29)
Reported landmine awareness education for children (n=21)	12	(57)
Experiences of Physical Abuse by Taliban Officials		
Self or family member detained/abused in Kabul over the past two years	26	(68)
Self (n=21)	7	(27)
Family member (n=21)	19	(73)
Reason detained/abused		
Dress code infraction (n=7 women)	6	(86)
Unaccompanied by appropriate chaperone (n=7 women)	1	(14)
Violation of beard/hair code (n=19 family members)	6	(32)
Ethnicity (n=19 family members)	6	(32)
Other (n=19 family members)	7	(36)
Type of Abuse		
Beating (n=26)	13	(50)
Incarceration (n=26)	6	(23)
Torture (n=26)	3	(12)
Other (n=26)	4	(15)

Characteristic	Response Number	(%)
Effects of Taliban Restrictions on Employment, Education and Freedom of Movement		
Reported lack of access to education in the past 2 years	38	(100)
Reported loss of employment due to Taliban restrictions	28	(74)
Reported restricted public/social activities in Kabul over the past two years	31	(81)
Attitudes Toward Women's Human Rights		
Reported women's human rights in Kabul deteriorated markedly over the past 2 years	37	(97)
The teachings of Islam do not restrict women's human rights	37	(97)

The Taliban's Violations of the Human Rights of Afghan Women

Restrictions on Access to Health Care

Before the Taliban took control of Afghanistan, health care services were available to women though a variety of organizations and facilities. A physician who had worked for seven years with an international assistance organization in Kabul described the availability of services:

> *In 1992, there were 32 Maternal and Child Health (MCH) Clinics and 4 contraceptive service clinics with good quality of care providing services to women in Kabul. Hospitals were free of charge. With the shift to the private sector since 1992, more than two-thirds of patients were treated in private clinics. The system shifted to curative care instead of preventive care. But, Kabul still had some governmentally supported hospitals and others supported by NGOs. Access was good, and male physicians could treat women.[152]*

A 50-year old Afghan nurse who worked as a head nurse in a hospital in Kabul and lost her job upon the Taliban's edict requiring women to leave paid employment, described the facilities at the time of Taliban takeover:

> *When I worked as a head nurse, my hospital did not have the new and modern technology, but we had the necessary medical tools and equipment. We had qualified female and male doctors. There was no segregation of health care providers and patients. Female nurses took care of male patients and male doctors treated female patients[153]*

---

[152] PHR Interview, H5, Kabul,Afghanistan

[153] PHR Interview, P15, Pakistan.

In January 1997, Taliban officials announced a policy of segregating men and women into separate hospitals.[154] This regulation was not strictly enforced until September 1997, when the Ministry of Public Health ordered all hospitals in Kabul to suspend medical services to the city's half million women at all but one, poorly-equipped clinic for women.[155]

The temporary Rabia Balkhi facility was designated the sole facility available to women. At that time the facility had 35 beds and no clean water, electricity, surgical equipment, X-ray machines, suction, or oxygen.[156] All female hospital personnel, including female physicians, nurses, pharmacists and technicians, also were banned from working in Kabul's 22 hospitals. After two months of negotiations with International Committee of the Red Cross officials, the Taliban reversed the policy and agreed to re-admit women into most hospitals and permit female hospital staff to work.[157]

On June 25, 1998 the Taliban reissued and amplified an edict forbidding physicians to treat women who are not accompanied by an appropriate male relative.[158] Also, the public baths for women have been ordered closed, eliminating what was once an important facility for women's hygiene and health.

One woman who lost her position as head nurse in a Kabul hospital reported that she never regained employment even after female health workers were granted permission to work.[159] One reason for the continuing limitations on employment among female health care providers is the brutal harassment they, like other woman, receive just by being out of their home. An Afghan physician described the effort to work at a clinic:

I now restrict my actions quite a bit, despite the fact that I am working in a clinic and leave the house every day. I am always worried about getting arrested or beaten. Working outside the house, even though we have permission from the Ministry of Health, is still a big risk. The Taliban are very unpredictable. One day the religious police may stop me on the street and ask where I am going. At that point, the fact that

---

[154] *Country Report on Human Rights, Supra*, 3.

[155] Block, M. "Kabul's Health Apartheid."*Supra*, 4.

[156] "Consequences of the new public health policy decisions regarding female health care in Kabul, Afghanistan," A briefing paper by Médecins sans Frontières, September 1997.

[157] Taliban's reportedly reverses hospital ban on women. *Australian Broadcasting Corporation*. November 26, 1997.

[158] From January 1997 on, Taliban prohibited women from seeing male doctors without a male chaperone, but women did go to hospitals unaccompanied. The new edict makes it clear that unaccompanied visits to clinics and hospitals are prohibited.

[159] PHR Interview, P15, Pakistan.

I have "permission" may mean nothing to him; he can beat me or ha-
rass me or arrest me at his whim. Every day, I leave my house and I
pray that I might get back home safely at the end of the day.[160]

On one occasion, the PHR researcher was informed about the cancel-
lation of her visit at one of the foreign NGO-supported clinics. She was
told that a few hours before her visit, Taliban religious police entered the
clinic and beat a dozen female health workers in front of their ex-patriate
colleagues. The reason for the beatings was, reportedly, a male ex-patriate physician had given a briefing about the activities of the clinic to the
employees, including the ex-patriates and Afghan women workers.

Another woman described drastic measures taken by the Taliban:

[The Taliban] beat my husband and myself, because we were work-
ing in the same clinic, and they wanted me to shut down the clinic
and not work. When I tried to reason with them, they beat me and
told me that they would hang me if I showed up again in the clinic.
   As a consequence, she and her husband shut down the clinic
"within twenty-four hours," stopped working as physicians in
Kabul and eventually came to Pakistan. Neither of them are cur-
rently employed. "We are nearly losing losing our minds staying in
this small room hoping that some clinic will accept my husband or
me even as an assistant to be able to work.[161]

As a result of the Taliban's edicts, the women of Afghanistan are denied access to health care services.[162] A physician employed by a humanitarian organization described the impact of the changes:

With the arrival of Taliban, however, the whole private sector was
shut down, especially for women doctors. This was a major blow to
the female and MCH care services, as I would estimate that up to
90 percent of women had relied on the private sector before the Tal-
iban movement gained power. The effect was more significant with
the closing of major hospitals to women.[163]

An internist stated that when Taliban authorities shut down most of
the health services for women and transferred all of the women into one
facility, dozens of ill women were sent home without a treatment plan or
medications. As a result some women were permanently disabled, some

---

[160] PHR Interview, K15, Kabul, Afghanistan

[161] PHR Interview, P3, Pakistan.

[162] In addition to investigating discrimination against women, PHR received reports that
some women were denied treatment because they were among the Hazara minority.
PHR Interview, K20, Kabul, Afghanistan.

[163] PHR Interview, H8 Kabul, Afghanistan.

women died of lack of treatment, and many had to suffer from their problems and pain without receiving medical attention. She said, "I treated several women at my home. Some patients who knew my address showed up at my door. I had to see them. Unfortunately, some of them I just couldn't treat at home. I don't know what happened to them after I came here [Pakistan].[164]

Another Afghan physician stressed that non-governmental organizations had increased support for maternal and child health clinics with improved standards of care that are open to women. Other respondents, however, noted the continued dearth of more specialized facilities for women. A physician who had been in Kabul for 17 months with an assistance organization noted:

> *Two years ago women [in Kabul] had access to at least four major surgical hospitals, five medical hospitals and three obstetrical facilities. In April, 1997 Jamhuriat Hospital, a surgical and medical hospital, was closed to women. In September, 1997, Wazir Akbar Khan, Karte Seh Surgical and Medical, Aliabad, Maiwand, and Avicenna Emergency and Chest all closed to women. At that time, a new women's hospital was started but its facilities were poor with too few, inadequately trained staff. While in November 1997, Wazir Akbar Khan and Karte Seh Surgical and Medical did reopen services to women, the other hospitals remain with very little or no access for women.[165]*

Paradoxically, despite the decline in traumatic injuries from shelling, and the availability of beds in hospitals, the quality of care has also deteriorated dramatically. Physicians and other health providers have left the country, medical supplies have become unavailable and adulterated medications are used with alarming frequency. An Afghan pharmacist described the situation:

> *The quality of health care has changed over the past two years. Almost all experienced and qualified physicians have left the country. Doctors working in the public hospitals are not paid enough and therefore, their mind is not on their patients' care. Some of them have to work another job in order to provide a living for their family. The quality of medicine is outrageously bad. Most of the drugs in the market are imported from Pakistan. There is no control or analysis of the imported medications before they are distributed in the market. I found chickpea powder inside capsules of Ampicillin. Most of the drugs are fake.[166]*

---

[164] PHR Interview, P14, Pakistan

[165] PHR Interview, H5, Kabul, Afghanistan

[166] PHR Interview, K16, Kabul, Afghanistan

An Afghan pediatrician confirmed this state of affairs:

The majority of hospitals have no medical equipment and tools. The drugs are very expensive and ineffective. Incentives for the health centers that are funded by foreign NGOs are OK, but public clinics have almost non-existent incentives for their medical staff. The salary of a doctor is equivalent to $5 per month. Salaries are not paid regularly. There are very few qualified and experienced doctors. The training for medical doctors is very poor. Most qualified doctors have immigrated to Pakistan or Iran. There is no training for the new doctors due to lack of medical facilities, equipment and tools, qualified trainers and medical personnel.[167]

A 35-year old professional woman described what she had seen:

The quality of health care services has changed a lot in the past two years. There are no qualified doctors, no medication, and no medical equipment in the hospitals. The patients are not treated properly. There is very little attention to patients. I witnessed one patient who was in desperate need of some pain medication but there was no pain medication. There is a great need for experienced doctors, more hospital facilities, blood banks, and medicine.[168]

One physician described her jailing by Taliban authorities:

One day [in June 1997] a few other Afghan women colleagues and I were stopped [by Taliban police] on the way to work, and our driver was questioned. Then all of us were jailed for three days. They made us feel that if we were caught again the punishment would be severe. That was it for me. My husband and I decided to leave Kabul and come to Pakistan.[169]

Another woman explained that patients have to buy everything, including their own IV fluids and syringes for injections.[170]

As PHR learned firsthand, notwithstanding the Taliban's promise to restore some medical services for women, hospital access remains grossly inadequate for women in Kabul. PHR toured the Rabia Balkhi facility and documented the poor conditions there. The hospital did not have running water, the building had very little medical and surgical equipment, no medication, gloves, and no proper sterilization system. All it appeared to have were beds.

---

[167] PHR Interview, K19, Kabul, Afghanistan

[168] PHR Interview, K14, Kabul, Afghanistan

[169] PHR Interview, P14, Pakistan.

[170] PHR Interview, P8, Pakistan.

The patients in Rabia Balkhi facility complained about lack of care, indicating that they had been there for many days and had been seen and treated by no one. One woman complained of abdominal distress, said that she had not been attended to in ten days, and indicated that her pain was worsening. Despite consistent reports by Afghan women of the inadequacy of health services for women, a Taliban administrator in the Rabia Balkhi facility told PHR that "women were receiving excellent care, and stated that the Rabia Balkhi facility saw some 1,000 outpatients per day.[171] She added that the "Taliban have not violated women's rights. I am the female staff of the Ministry of Public Health. The Taliban Minister of Public Health sees to both male and female health services equally. It is not correct that Taliban have abused females' rights. Taliban are much kinder toward women than any other government in Afghanistan…they give me a vacation and respect me a lot."

PHR visited the only maternity hospital in Kabul, Maiwand, and found very poor facilities there as well. There were six or seven beds to a room and in one room two patients shared one bed. One woman was losing her child because of Rh incompatibility because no antigen was available. Several women interviewed by the researcher were experiencing abnormal bleeding during pregnancy. Some were given a prescription but they had not purchased it because they couldn't afford it; other women had been at the hospital for days and had no treatment at all.

Afghan women reported the consequences of restricted access to facilities based on gender. Many women and their children have no access to health care facilities, even in cases of dire emergencies. One Kabul woman reported:

> Women are not admitted in several hospitals. My niece had severe diarrhea. We took her to Aliabad hospital, but they refused to see her. They asked us to take her to a private doctor, but we couldn't afford a private doctor's fee. She barely survived.[172]

An Afghan pediatrician reported:

> Four months ago, two of my former colleagues were injured in car accident. One had trauma of neck and the other was also seriously injured. They were refused treatment in five hospitals because they were female.[173]

Another Afghan woman, now living in Pakistan, reported that she knew a woman who died of appendicitis after having been turned away

---

[171] PHR Interview, H9, Kabul, Afghanistan

[172] PHR Interview, K4, Kabul, Afghanistan.

[173] PHR Interview, K19, Kabul, Afghanistan

by two hospitals.[174] Two interviewees recounted the experiences of women who had diabetes, but were turned down in an effort to obtain insulin at a clinic. They each died soon thereafter.[175]

These restrictions have a profound effect on pregnant women. The health professionals PHR interviewed cited women's reproductive health as a particularly critical area of concern. Even before the rise of the Taliban, maternal mortality rates in Afghanistan were among the highest in the world.[176] More recent UN surveys (which are limited by the current constraints on accurate data collection) estimate that only ten percent of Afghan women receive any type of formal prenatal or maternal care and less than six percent of deliveries are attended by trained birth attendants.[177] And as one physician noted:

> *Under current policies, this situation will only get worse. Already there are a limited number of female obstetricians that women are supposed to see exclusively. And now the training of more women health professionals has been halted completely, so there is no way there will be women doctors for future generations.*[178]

Afghan women are thus caught in the paradoxical bind of being compelled to seek care only from female providers at the same time that governmental decrees ensure a dwindling supply of such providers. Health professionals from Afghanistan see the effects in the lives — and deaths — of women. A nurse who has since left Afghanistan reported that many women died at home during labor[179] and an Afghan pharmacist who remains in the country explained:

> *It is very difficult for pregnant women since male doctors are prohibited from seeing pregnant women and performing delivery. A lot of pregnant women die at home and in hospital and clinics.*[180]

One woman now living in Pakistan reported that in December, 1997, she had a kidney infection but could not get attention in a clinic because she could not find a female doctor. Luckily, she obtained medical attention in Pakistan.[181]

---

[174] PHR Interview, K15, Kabul, Afghanistan.

[175] PHR Interview, P4, Pakistan

[176] UN figures for 1996, the most recent year available, give a rate of 1700 per 100,000 live births. 1998 UN Consolidated Appeal,.p.8

[177] 1998 UN Consolidated Appeal, p.31

[178] PHR Interview, H3, Kabul, Afghanistan

[179] PHR Interview, P15, Pakistan

[180] PHR Interview, K16, Kabul, Afghanistan

[181] PHR Interview, P5, Pakistan.

Restrictions on cross-gender treatment extend to children. One woman reported:

> Eight months ago, my two-and-a-half year old daughter died from diarrhea. She was refused treatment by the first hospital that we took her to. The second hospital mistreated her (they refused to provide intravenous fluids or antibiotics because of her Hazara ethnicity, according to the respondent). Her body was handed to me and her father in the middle of the night. With her body in my arms, we left the hospital. It was curfew time and we had a long way to get home. We had to spend the night inside a destroyed house among the rubble. In the morning we took my dead baby home but we had no money for her funeral.[182]

A physician PHR interviewed reported that a female child died of measles because the authorities didn't allow a male doctor to visit the children's ward, which is located within a designated female ward of a local hospital.[183] One nurse who had been working in Kabul for one year related an incident that occurred in early 1998:

> I recently referred a child—a boy—with a facial tumor to Maiwand Hospital to see a surgeon. As the only possible caretaker for this child was his mother, his mother accompanied him to the appointment. Even though the child was a boy, both he and his mother were not allowed to enter the consultation room, since the doctor was a male working in a male ward.[184]

When women do gain access to male health care providers, proper examination and treatment is all but impossible because men are not permitted to see or touch women's bodies:

> But even [when a women is accompanied by a male chaperone] the treatment is limited to office consultation and over-the-clothing examination. Male doctors are not allowed to do surgical procedures, even if a patient's life is at stake.[185]

These restrictions on medical examinations of sick or injured women have reached extreme dimensions. PHR interviewed a male physician and asked how he would treat an ailing woman patient. He indicated that in some cases, a male relative could point on his own body to places where the patient felt pain; and he would prescribe medication for the

---

[182] PHR Interview K6, Kabul, Afghanistan.

[183] PHR Interview, K15, Kabul, Afghanistan.

[184] PHR Interview, H7, Kabul, Afghanistan

[185] Id.

male relative to procure for her. In other cases, the doctor would examine a woman through her clothing, not touching her skin.[186] A dentist assured PHR that he did see female patients, but was unable to explain how he was able to examine their teeth under the all-enveloping *burqa*. Though visibly frightened, he eventually acknowledged that he did upon occasion lift the veil and treat women, but only if his own lookouts posted outside the clinic gave the "all clear" sign. When asked what would happen if he were caught treating a woman, he answered straightforwardly that police would beat him and the patient, and likely close his office and throw him in jail.[187]

The result is that obtaining health care has become an ordeal. A nurse described how truly difficult access has become:

> There are a lot of problems for women. The [NGO] clinics are available but there is always a long wait before getting to see a doctor. It took me two days to get in and see a nurse practitioner. I walked a long way to this clinic, but at the end of the day I didn't get to see a doctor and I had to come back the next day at 6 o'clock in the morning and wasn't seen until noon. This is what most women have to go through in order to see a clinician at the international MCH clinics. In this city of almost one half a million women citizens, there is only one obstetrics hospital. To see a private doctor you need to have money to pay a fee. I had a kidney infection twice but I couldn't seek treatment because I couldn't afford to pay for the prescription. You are refused treatment if you can't pay the fee.[188]

Another woman described the travails of trying to obtain health care:

> I am unable to get medical treatment, because I can't afford to pay the doctor's fee or the transportation fare to get to a clinic. At the free [female] clinics, the wait is very long. Sometimes, you have to wait all day and then, often, you are still not seen by the end of the day. I don't have anyone to [accompany me] and to watch my children, so it is very difficult for me to go to the free clinic and wait all day.[189]

Finally, for those woman who manage to make their way into the system, to survive long waits, to find a chaperone, to get across the city, more

---

[186] PHR Interview, H9, Kabul, Afghanistan.

[187] PHR Interview, H12, Kabul, Afghanistan.

[188] PHR Interview, K3, Kabul, Afghanistan.

[189] PHR Interview, K4, Kabul, Afghanistan.

[190] Fortunately for some women and girls, the Taliban have deviated from ideological purity when it comes to health care for its own family members. The best health care for women in Kabul (albeit inferior to that which is available for men) can be found at the 400-bed military hospital. When the wife of a Taliban official needed surgery and could not obtain it because of the Taliban's restrictions, the authorities invited Afghanistan's top female surgeon to establish a 100-bed women's section within the campus of the 400-bed Kabul military hospital.

travails may await them. Taliban guards[190] are ever present in medical facilities and intervene at will on behalf of the religious police (Department for the Propagation of Virtue and the Suppression of Vice). Nurses are beaten when not covered completely, and women often fear to even venture from their homes to seek health care for themselves or their children.[191]

Prohibition on Work and the Impoverishment of Women

With the exception of a small percentage of positions available as health workers and as surveyors with international aid organizations,[192] Afghan women are not permitted to work. This prohibition exists notwithstanding the dire circumstances of hundreds of thousands of women widowed by wars lasting two decades and a long tradition of work, including professionalism, among Afghan women. Before the Taliban,women worked as teachers, nurses, physicians, pharmacists, and held other essential jobs in society. Now, most are relegated to unemployment and destitution, and begging is, for many, the only option. PHR's researcher saw many women begging on the streets of Kabul.

One widow explained her plight:

Women are literally forced to beg on the streets. For most widows who have nobody close to look after them, begging is the only way to feed their children.[193]

Another woman reported:

I have economic problems, mental distress, loneliness and a lot of health problems. Five months after my husband's death, my younger brother was injured by another rocket attack in Kabul city. In the last two years, my sufferings have doubled due to the harsh and strict policies of Taliban on people in Kabul, in particular on women. As a widow, I have no support system in this society and I am about to lose my mind. . . . It is worse than two years ago. The high cost of living is depressing; you can't even afford to buy wheat, flour, cooking oil, etc. . . . I need to work to support myself and family, but there are no jobs for women. With no husband, no job, no other source of income, the economic situation is bad for me. I barely survive without any support and income. There are beatings for showing up in public without a male chaperone or showing your face. Worst of all is not being allowed to work. How can a widow survive like this?[194]

---

[191] Health Care Under the Taliban, *The Lancet*, Vol. 349, April 26, 1997.

[192] Even these woman are not immune from the discriminatory employment policies of the Taliban. One health worker reported that the Taliban tried to demote her from a supervisory position at a facility supported by an international NGO because she was a woman. PHR Interview K19, Kabul, Afghanistan.

[193] PHR Interview, P4, Pakistan.

[194] PHR Interview, K1, Kabul, Afghanistan

Another woman described her economic hopelessness:

We are ten times worse off than we were two years ago. We are with-out jobs, and don't have a regular income. And with the high prices for food and any household goods, we are in a terrible economic sit-uation. We prefer the rocket attacks and the fighting to the current situation under Taliban. A rocket or a bomb may kill all members of a family at once, but this is a slow death, which is more painful.[195]

The lack of income deprives families of food and of fuel in winter. A woman whose brothers were imprisoned by the Communist regime and who lost an uncle and two cousins in a rocket attack, and suffers from ill health herself, must now cope, too, with grinding poverty:

There are no jobs here, and thus we have no income. We have noth-ing to eat. We have no money to buy any groceries, and the prices are extremely high. We don't eat meat, fruits or vegetables for months at a time. In the winter, we are very cold. The situation is getting worse...the non-stop war, the poor economy, and our poor health status all makes women's lives very difficult here in Kabul.[196]

For many, economic deprivation comes atop the suffering of having lost husbands to war. An Afghan widow who finally fled to Pakistan de-scribed her effort to survive in Kabul after the death of her husband:

He was sitting in his office when a bullet passed through the window and hit him in his heart. After his death our home was destroyed by a rocket, and we moved to a different part of the city. I suffered a lot from the loss of my husband. My children were young when their fa-ther was killed. The pressure was too much on me: I had to be a fa-ther and a mother for them. I was working two jobs, and we had an okay living until 1996 when another disaster happened. The Taliban took me out of work and my daughters out of school. This was un-bearable and sickening for me and my entire family. I almost lost my sanity, and I did not have anyone to support me financially. ...Without a source of income and with the dramatic rise in prices, I didn't have a way to support my family. If I hadn't left, I would have gone crazy[197]

Similar experiences were reported by others:

This was the most bitter part of my life, losing the man of my life. I wanted to die too. But because of my child, I had to live to take care of him. Today, I still live in turmoil and sorrow and mentally don't

---

[195] PHR Interview, K6, Kabul, Afghanistan

[196] PHR Interview, K13, Kabul, Afghanistan

[197] PHR Interview, P5, Pakistan.

*feel normal. I had to leave my home after the Taliban took over
Kabul. They took away the only thing that kept me from losing my
mind—my job and my income....I was sent home from work like many
other women. I lost my income, my future, and almost my sanity.*[198]

When combined with the difficulties of access to health care, a lack of
income makes life unbearable for many women of Kabul. A pediatrician
who considered herself fortunate to be working described the woman
she sees each day:

*Women are facing a lot of difficulties. These difficulties include eco-
nomic hardship, social restrictions and health problems. The majority of women are mothers. They suffer because they can't provide
for their children. They don't have a job, and of those who are married, their husbands don't have a job. Every day, I have two or three
women who come to me and ask for a job. They cry and tell me
about their difficulties and the intolerable living conditions.*[199]

Restrictions on the Education of Girls and Women

Before the Taliban took control of Kabul, schools were coeducational and
women accounted for seventy percent of all teachers, about fifty percent
of civil servants, and forty percent of medical doctors.[200] One of the first
edicts issued by the Taliban regime when it rose to power was to prohibit
girls and women from attending school. Humanitarian groups initiated
projects to replace through philanthropy what prior governments had afforded as a right to both sexes.[201] Hundreds of girls' schools were established in private homes, and thousands of women and girls were taught to
sew and weave. On June 16, 1998, the Taliban ordered the closing of
more than 100 privately funded schools where thousands of young
women and girls were receiving training in skills that would have helped
them support their families. The Taliban issued new rules for non-governmental organizations providing the schooling: education must be limited to girls up to the age of eight, and restricted to the *Qur'an.*[202]

---

[198] PHR Interview, P11, Pakistan

[199] PHR Interview, K19, Kabul, Afghanistan

[200] *E/CN.4/1997/59, Supra,* 22

[201] Historically, Afghan women had an illiteracy rate of over 80%, but it was not based on
legal prohibitions on their attendance in school. Afghanistan had free public education
for all before the Taliban, but facilities for schooling of both boys and girls were poor
and scarce in rural areas. And conservative families often restricted girls' access to public education.

[202] 100 Girls' Schools in Afghan Capital Are Ordered Shut, *The New York Times,* June 17,
1998. (Associated Press, June 16, 1998.)

One young woman explained the situation:

> *The quality of education is obviously changed for females. Women are not allowed to start or complete their education. Two years ago I graduated from Kabul University, but now the university door is closed to all female students-Afghan women have no rights today. They are all walking deads.*[203]

The despair that afflicts women prevented from working thus extends to girls equally trapped in hopelessness and confinement in the home. Mothers suffer as well. One mother stated, " Both of my daughters were locked at home and not allowed to continue their college educations. We had to cover our windows and stay at home all day long. No radio, no television, no music—my daughters were about to go crazy."[204] PHR's interviews revealed that women feared the limited opportunities for their children, specifically denial of education to girl children. Poor and uneducated women spoke with particular urgency of their desire to obtain education for children, and saw health care, schooling, and protection of human rights as a key towards achieving a better future. Those hopes now seem shattered. As one physician put it, "Thousands of young girls and women are hopeless, sitting at home with an incomplete education. And this is not because of the teachings of Islam, it is what Taliban are imposing on people."[205]

Restrictions on Freedom of Movement and Physical Abuse for Non-Compliance

Afghan women are virtual prisoners in their homes. The Taliban have issued edicts requiring women appearing on the street to wear a *burqa* and prohibiting women from travelling without a male chaperone. These edicts are often brutally and arbitrarily enforced by Taliban "religious police" (the Department for the Propagation of Virtue and the Suppression of Vice) usually in the form of summary, public beatings.[206]

The *burqa* is no ordinary garment. It is a heavy envelopment covering the entire body, with a narrow slit covered by mesh for the eyes to see through. Some women choose to wear a *burqa* or wear one to satisfy their husband. For others it is suffocating. It is certainly the case that

---

[203] PHR Interview, K16, Kabul, Afghanistan.

[204] PHR Interview, P6, Pakistan.

[205] PHR Interview, K15, Kabul, Afghanistan. The Taliban restrictions also are affecting boys because of the absence of teachers and the widespread poverty that prevents families from even buying a pencil and paper for their boys. PHR Interview, K16, Kabul, Afghanistan.

[206] William Maley, "Health Care under the Taliban, Letter, *The Lancet*, September 6, 1977.

there are areas of conservatism in Afghanistan where women have traditionally worn the veil. But a draconian dress code has never before been imposed by the authorities and punishment for violations has never been imposed by the state.

One Afghan women complained:

> *Taliban are violating our rights completely. I have had to change my behavior a lot in public. I must wear a burqa when going outside the house. I have a baby to carry with me, and it is very difficult to do that with a burqa covering your face..I own an old burqa, which has holes in it. Most women can't afford to buy a new burqa, yet they are forced to wear them.*[207]

Another woman described her experience with a *burqa*:

> *The burqa is another reason for not wanting to go outside the house. I am not used to wearing the burqa and it is a risk for me every time I wear it. I can fall and break my leg or my neck, also, I don't think it is good for my eyesight.*[208]

Women begged PHR's researcher to send them some *burqas* from the United States so that they could go out on the streets.[209]

Another woman explained how her father's life became in danger because she was not wearing a *burqa*:

> *I was inside a taxi with my sick father, taking him to the hospital. I didn't have a burqa on, since I did not even own one. The Taliban police stopped the taxi and almost beat my sick father and the driver. The taxi driver begged them to let us go, since he had a sick man in his car. They verbally insulted me and told me to go home and cover my face before taking my father to the hospital. I had to go home and borrow a neighbor's burqa. Only then could I take my father to the hospital. I don't have a brother, and my only uncle is an amputee. Thus, I have to be the one to take my father to the doctor.*[210]

The feeling that wearing the *burqa* is injurious to health is not mere opinion. Two physicians described the danger. An Afghan pediatrician explained:

---

[207] PHR Interview, K8, Kabul, Afghanistan

[208] PHR Interview, K19 , Kabul, Afghanistan

[209] In Kabul, a very cheap burqa costs approximately $9.00 U.S.—which is much more than most Afghan women can now afford.

[210] PHR Interview, P8, Pakistan

Walking in a burqa is hard; it has so many heath hazards. It causes poor vision, impaired hearing, skin rashes, headaches, itching of the scalp and loss of hair. Wearing a burqa also causes depression in women. You can't see well and there is a risk of falling or getting hit by a car. Shopping is problematic for women, since we can't see the items very well from under the burqa. Also, for women with asthma and hypertension, wearing a burqa is very unhealthy.[211]

The penalty for not wearing a *burqa* is a beating. The woman of Afghanistan know this very well, often through cruel experience — and it is terrifying:

We can't go out shopping, we can't go to the doctor, we can't leave home without head to toe cover. Any slight divergence from the dress code results in beating—we live in terror.[212]

Another woman described the experience of her mother-in-law:

I was with my mother-in-law shopping at a fabric store. A Taliban police walked in and hit my mother-in-law with his stick. The reason? She had her face uncovered. She was trying to look at the quality of the material she was going to buy. It is very difficult to see from under a burqa the color and quality of anything you may want to purchase. The Taliban militia man then threatened both of us, ordered us to leave the store, and verbally insulted both of us.[213]

Even young girls and old women do not escape the violence inflicted on them for not wearing a *burqa*. One woman interviewed described an incident involving her eight-year-old-sister, who was beaten by the Taliban religious police for not wearing a *burqa*:

She was frightened by that incident and now she experiences psychological distress. For example, she is afraid of leaving the house, she has bad dreams, and she is very upset and depressed.[214]

Another described what happened to her great aunt:

My mother's aunt, an elderly woman, was flogged by a Taliban militia member because her ankle was showing. She was beaten with a metal cable, and her leg was broken. She is here in Pakistan now for treatment.[215]

---

[211] PHR Interview, K19, Kabul, Afghanistan

[212] PHR Interview, K20, Kabul, Afghanistan

[213] PHR Interview, P10, Pakistan.

[214] PHR Interview, K1, Kabul, Afghanistan

[215] PHR Interview, P19, Pakistan

Five of the humanitarian workers interviewed had personally seen authorities beat or physically abuse women in public for infringements such as not wearing the *burqa* or being in public alone. The social worker with an international organization in early 1998 recounted the following:

> *For the past six months neither I nor my staff have heard of or seen any woman being beaten. Within the first two months of the Taliban's arrival in Kabul, however, two women in my office were detained. One was severely beaten on the head and now cannot hear from one ear—though the sub-station head of police responsible for this was himself beaten and demoted because of this incident.*[216]

One physician told of female colleagues who had been beaten with a stick or leather strap for walking across an enclosed hospital compound in 1997 without a *burqa* on (although they had their heads and shoulders covered with a *chador*). Another told of a relative of his organization's security guard who had her wrist broken with a metal stick for not wearing a burqa. Two of the female physicians PHR interviewed had themselves been beaten and verbally abused by Taliban authorities for perceived inappropriate attire.

Afghan women can no longer walk the streets unaccompanied by a man. Many women described themselves as prisoners in their own home out of fear or because they cannot afford a *burqa*. One woman described her life:

> *My activity is restricted, but little in comparison to those women who use to work outside the home. I didn't work before. However, I now follow the strict dress code when going outside the house and the most difficult thing for me is having to have a male chaperone every time I go out.*[217]

The constant fear of what awaits them on the street for the slightest offense — or perceived offense — perpetuates the feeling of imprisonment:

> *I have now restricted my activity in public quite a bit since the Taliban issued these edicts. Before, I was able to go out freely, but now I worry about getting beaten by the religious police. My mother-in-law is affected by the Taliban policy too, because she used to work as a cleaning woman before but now she is without a job.*[218]

---

[216] PHR Interview, H6, Kabul, Afghanistan

[217] PHR Interview, K1, Kabul, Afghanistan

[218] PHR Interview, K4, Kabul, Afghanistan

Another Afghan woman summarized the impact of Taliban edicts on her:

> *We undergo public beatings, we have no right to express our opinions, and we have no right to employment, or freedom of movement. Women and girls are not allowed to go to school due to Taliban edicts. I have changed my activities quite a bit. I am stuck at home, with no job and no social life. I don't have a male chaperone and when I need to go someplace it is very difficult for me to leave the house knowing that I might get detained and beaten for appearing in public alone. I don't like to leave the house unless it is necessary.*[219]

Even those women fortunate enough to retain employment in the health field with an international organization remained intimidated and fearful. A pharmacy worker describes how these restrictions on movement have brought fear and depression to her life:

> *It is very hard for me to move around: transportation is difficult. I am not allowed to drive a car, ride on a taxi alone, or ride the city buses. I can only ride the city buses designated for females only, which has a very long wait. The bus will not leave until it is filled up with women and that can take hours. We must wear a burqa and undergo beatings if we don't. I can't go to the market or a shop to buy something I need easily and without following the dress code. It is difficult to buy good quality stuff because we can't see well from under the burqa. I worked before and recently I got lucky and found a job as a pharmacy worker. If not for my job, I would get depressed and die.*[220]

Health Status in the Context of Human Rights Violations Against Women

Women's Perceptions of their Health

A very high percentage of Afghan women who participated in PHR's health and human rights survey reported a decline in their physical and mental health and the presence of multiple specific symptoms since the beginning of the Taliban regime. PHR's interviews confirmed that the perceived deterioration in health status largely stems from the human rights violations described above. An Afghan physician provided an overview of the state of women's health in Kabul today:

> *Women live under severe restrictions. Most widows can't provide for food or clothing for their children. They beg on the streets. They must for there are no jobs or education for females. The living conditions are extremely poor. Children lack a nutritious diet, the rate*

---

[219] PHR Interview, K18, Kabul, Afghanistan

[220] PHR interview, K16, Kabul, Afghanistan

of TB is increasing, and there is a high prevalence of infectious diseases among women and children. We're seeing an increasing number of birth defects among newborns, and women are not breastfeeding as much. Mental illness is very common, as is economic hardship among most people, especially women in Kabul.[221]

These observations were confirmed by the experiences of women PHR interviewed. One woman described her health:

Three months ago I was diagnosed with TB. In the beginning I was coughing. The house was cold and I couldn't afford to buy firewood, and just thought that it was a common cold. The examination then showed I was positive. I have other problems as well, such as stomach upset from too much acid, leg pain, abnormal periods, anemia and mental distress. My sister is also in poor health.[222]

A woman with seven children, two of whom suffer from malnutrition, and whose home was destroyed in a rocket attack, reported:

We are the poorest of the poor. I am tired of living this way. We are struggling for survival. The living condition has dramatically changed in comparison to two years ago. Now, there are no jobs available, and thus there is no business and no income for families. We have lost everything. I am now forced to sell my belongings in order to survive. My husband is repairing old shoes, but the business is bad and thus he doesn't make any money. . . .

My health is worse compared to two years ago, primarily due to our terrible economic situation. . . . I suffer from abdominal pain, anemia, a rapid heartbeat, fatigue and back pain.[223]

Another woman, who had lost her 13-year-old daughter and 32-year-old brother to a rocket attack, described her experience:

It is like living in hell. If we find wheat flour, we can't find cooking oil; if we find tea, there is no sugar. Everyone in the city lives in misery. We all look sick and malnourished. I got a back injury from a rocket attack a few years ago and have had problems since. And after my child was delivered at Malali hospital [the only obstetrical hospital in Kabul], I developed an infection and now have considerable discomfort in my lower abdominal area. . . . Women have very little access to the healthcare. For example, I myself have been refused treatment. I don't have money to pay for the care I need for treating my current problem.[224]

---

[221] *Id.*

[222] PHR Interview, K10, Kabul, Afghanistan

[223] PHR Interview, K4, Kabul, Afghanistan

[224] PHR Interview, K8, Kabul, Afghanistan

And another woman told PHR:

I experienced emotional distress when my husband was killed....but I am worse now. In the past year, I have more mental and emotional problems. I faint when I get upset about something. I have had abnormal bleeding for the past year. My entire body aches—my back, lower abdomen, legs, shoulders and arms— and I don't sleep at night.[225]

The mental and emotional impact of the deprivations and human rights violations among the women of Kabul are, if anything, even more severe than somatic problems. The frequency of PTSD, major depression, and significant symptoms of anxiety among the study participants well exceeded that found in refugee populations receiving mental health services in the United States.[226] The combination of years of war and the Taliban occupation almost certainly have profoundly affected these women's mental health [227] A 47-year old former health worker, now widowed with five children, summed it up:

The loss of my husband and brother, the intense fighting and bombing of the city, the rising cost of living, not being able to work outside the house to earn an income, witnessing public executions, amputations and beatings, poverty and increased numbers of beggars on the streets, watching my daughters suffer from not being allowed to complete their education, among other things, has driven me close to insanity. I can't sleep well at nights. I nearly faint every time I hear a loud noise. I lose my patience quickly, and sometimes I think this life is not worth living.[228]

It is the brutality of the regime, and the constant fear that accompanies it that may have the greatest impact on women's health. One woman re-

---

[225] PHR Interview, K1, Kabul, Afghanistan

[226] See Kinzie JD, Boehnlein JK, Leung PK, Moore LJ, Riley C Smith D. The prevalence of post-traumatic stress disorder and its clinical significance among Southeast Asian refugees. *Am J Psychiatry.* 1990; 147:913-7; Mollica RF, Wyshak G, Lavelle J. The psychological impact of trauma and torture on Southeast Asian refugees. *Am J Psychiatry.* 1987;144:1567-1572; Westermeyer J, Vang TF, Neider J. A comparison of refugees using and not using Operational Psychiatry. 1983; 14:36-41; and Mghir R, Freed W, Raskin A, Katon W. Depression and post-traumatic stress disorder among a community sample of adolescent and young adult Afghan refugees. *J Nerv Ment Dis.* 1995; 183:24-30.

[227] Children are also traumatized by such sights and experiences. During an interview at the home of a woman several days after a public beheading, a young boy in the home was continually crying. When the researcher asked why he was crying, the child, who had actually been forced to witness the execution, said that he was frightened because of the killings going on around him.

[228] PHR Interview, P12, Pakistan.

counted the mental agony she felt after the torture and imprisonment of her fiancé and the beating of her brother by the Taliban:

> *My fiancé was detained by the Taliban because of his ethnicity and has been in jail since then. I don't know if they tortured him, but I do know he was beaten. I saw his bloody shirt. I don't know whether he will come out alive...Now I am having all kinds of mental problems. I have very little sleep at night. I have bad dreams. I am always depressed and down. I get angry very easily, and I don't like loud noises.[229]*

She also said that a male acquaintance of hers was beaten "black and blue" for playing music during his wedding and her brother was beaten by Taliban police for not being at the mosque during prayer time.

A physician recalled her encounter with Taliban officials in her medical office:

> *In the first days of their [the Taliban's] arrival, the religious police from the Office of Prevention of Vice and Promotion of Virtue stormed into my office, threw things around, sent all of my patients away and ordered me to close the office right away. I asked them why were they so rude and why should I close my office. In response, one of them told me in a menacing tone, while he pointed to a tree outside the window, "You are a woman. Don't talk back to me, or I will bury you alive under that tree." Since that event, I have been ill mentally, emotionally, and physically. I can never forget what he told me. I can't sleep at night, and during the days I keep thinking about what he said to me.[230]*

A 56-year-old widow who lost her job when the Taliban came to power described the suffering she and her children experience and the consequences for their physical and mental health:

> *I have seen bloody bodies after a rocket attack in our neighborhood. [Since the Taliban came to power] I have seen women being punished on the street for not wearing burqas. I have fed my children only bread and water... I am watching my daughters suffer from not being able to complete their education [in Afghanistan]. All of these things are eating me up and I feel that mentally I am about to lose my mind... Both physically and mentally I have many problems—leg pain, back problems, rheumatic arthritis, hypertension, anxiety, and mental distress from prolonged stress. My daughter also has rheumatic arthritis and constantly complains of headaches. She does not like to go out and has become very down*

---

[229] PHR Interview, P16, Pakistan.

[230] PHR Interview, P14, Pakistan.

and depressed. My other children are in fair to good health, but they all suffer emotional and psychological problems. Before the Taliban I had back pain and hypertension, but everything else started in the past two years.[231]

A physician relayed the toll on her health:

My health has been ruined over the past two years. I have chronic fatigue, headaches, and depression. I am very tense, nervous, and feel like crying all of the time. My other family members have also developed psychological problems[232]

The absence of health statistics renders it impossible to learn the suicide rate among women in Kabul, but one woman PHR interviewed reported that parents have committed suicide because they can't feed their children and that young women who have lost hope are committing suicide.[233] In PHR's health and human rights survey, 21% of the 160 participants indicated that they had suicidal thoughts "quite often" or "extremely often".

The Limitations of Humanitarian Assistance

There are currently more than 40 international non-governmental organizations (NGOs) in addition to national governmental and United Nations agencies active in Afghanistan. Most of these organizations have focused on assisting vulnerable groups, with many development, health, and food distribution programs targeting women and their families. The increased limits on women's activities imposed by the Taliban regime have constrained program efforts to benefit women beyond the distribution of food and basic supplies. In response some NGOs, such as Save the Children-UK, which focused on education and health,[234] temporarily closed operations in Taliban-controlled areas. In 1996, United Nations agencies, following the lead of UNICEF, also stopped support for school education programs in areas of Afghanistan where governmental decrees denied girls access to schooling.[235]

International agencies have struggled to continue seeking means to address the needs of Afghan women in the context of the Taliban

---

[231] PHR Interview, P7, Pakistan

[232] PHR Interview, P14, Pakistan.

[233] PHR Interview, P10, Pakistan

[234] United Nations, *Afghanistan: An Enduring Tragedy*, Department of Humanitarian Affairs, May 1996, p. 5.

[235] *Id.*

regime's discriminatory, gender-based policies. How best to achieve this has been at the center of debate both within and among the international organizations working in Afghanistan[236] The United Nations High Commissioner for Refugees (UNHCR), the UN agency responsible for assisting refugees, the majority of whom are women, firmly enunciates an approach to the problem in its 1998 Programme Overview:

> *Constraints due to the conservative cultural environment have severely limited access, employment and assistance delivery for women in Afghanistan. Despite these obstacles, UNHCR maintains a strong determination to ensure that women be given a prominent role in the design of delivery of services. Programs which target women receive particular attention and include skills-training activities, income-generating projects and micro-credit group guaranteed loans for poor women and female-headed households. UNHCR works with local authorities to improve education and employment opportunities for women.[237]*

In the face of the Taliban regime's measures curtailing women's activities, UN and other international agencies continue to "see it as an essential part of their mandate to promote the participation of Afghan women in all aspects of the assistance programmes and to ensure that all projects benefit women as well as men."[238]

Notwithstanding this commitment, there exist severe restrictions in the humanitarian aid actually reaching Afghan women. In striking contrast to published reports indicating the successful disbursement of humanitarian assistance,[239] only 6% of respondents in our survey reported receiving any form of humanitarian assistance while living in Kabul. One physician said that "if it weren't for the humanitarian aid groups, most people in Kabul would have starved to death. At the same time, the level of assistance is not enough in comparison to other countries in conflict. Malnutrition is high among children and women."[240]

One explanation may be that Taliban gender restrictions interfere

---

[236] See the Department of Humanitarian Affairs report from 1997 for a full discussion of different United Nations agencies' divergent strategies for reconciling their program goals of supporting women's livelihoods and training with Taliban decrees.

[237] UNHCR, *1998 Global Appeal, Programme Overview for Afghanistan*, p. 134.

[238] United Nations, Department of Humanitarian Affairs, *Afghanistan: An Enduring Tragedy*, May 1996, p.6

[239] *E/CN.4/1996/64, Supra*, 29

[240] PHR Interview, P14, Pakistan.

with the delivery of humanitarian assistance to women.[241] Furthermore, edicts restricting women's mobility and their access to humanitarian aid offices clearly limit their access to assistance. Women are prohibited from entering a non-governmental organization's building, for example.

A Taliban decree of July 20, 1997 stated that women could no longer themselves pick up their food or other aid from distribution centers unless accompanied by a close male relative. Those most in need — widows — are particularly hard pressed by this requirement.

One widow stated:

> *The aid organizations have what I feel are ridiculous rules which exclude widows from necessary assistance. For example, if you are a widow and over 45 years of age, you are not eligible for aid. They assume that everyone over the age of 45 has a grown son who should support the family. Not thinking that even if these widows do have a grownup son, the may not have a job—there also aren't any jobs for men in the city. There is no business, there is no trade market, there is nothing to do.*[242]

Moreover, many women interviewed in the course of the PHR survey indicated that the local officials responsible for drawing up lists of those eligible for aid are corrupt and unresponsive. "All I know is that we don't receive any humanitarian assistance. Corruption is outrageous among the *Wakeels* [the person in charge of enlisting the needy families in each district to the aid organizations]. We have no money to bribe the *Wakeel* in our district in order to get on the list for assistance."[243]

Women we interviewed confirmed the difficulty of obtaining aid. One 19-year-old woman in Kabul, whose father was killed by a landmine and who, herself, was paralyzed by a rocket attack and suffers from tuberculosis, reported that she manages to receive medical care from an international agency, but that her mother gets no help from humanitarian aid for widows.[244]

PHR confirmed that many humanitarian organizations have strict rules that women must comply with before receiving assistance. Through interviews with Afghan women and humanitarian assistance workers, PHR learned that some humanitarian organizations conduct home surveys to assess eligibility for assistance. If, for example, a fam-

---

[241] *Country Report on Human Rights, Supra,*3.

[242] PHR Interview, P12, Pakistan.

[243] PHR Interview, K4, Kabul, Afghanistan.

[244] PHR Interview, K2, Kabul, Afghanistan.

ily owns household items, such as a carpet, radio, or furniture (regardless of condition), they may not be eligible for assistance until the family has liquidated these "assets". One Afghan physician summed up the problem of insufficient humanitarian assistance as follows: "while more aid organizations have come to Kabul over the last two years, it is not enough. The people of Afghanistan are desperate." [245]

Another important reason why Afghan women do not receive adequate humanitarian assistance is that women who flee Afghanistan under Taliban rule are not designated as refugees. Therefore, they are not entitled to assistance or protection by the United Nations High Commissioner for Refugees. The vast majority of women who migrate to host countries, such as Pakistan, resettle in cities such as Peshawar and Islamabad. Far fewer reside in refugee camps because they receive little or no assistance there. The systematic and egregious violations of women's human rights documented in this report clearly indicate that Afghan women have "well-founded fear of persecution" by the Taliban. The lack of assistance and protection under such circumstances unnecessarily adds to the suffering Afghan women fleeing gender-based persecution and should be remedied as soon as possible.

---

[245] PHR Interview, K17, Kabul, Afghanistan

V. APPLICATION OF RELEVANT INTERNATIONAL LAW

International Human Rights Law

PHR takes no position with respect to the religious or customary laws followed in any country, including Afghanistan, except insofar as particular interpretations or applications of such laws violate universally recognized human rights. A wide array of international treaties, declarations and resolutions govern aspects of women's health-related rights. The weight and status of these instruments vary under international law. For example, treaties are legally binding upon parties while declarations and resolutions carry only moral force. Nevertheless, in order to provide a sense of the breadth and depth of international consensus regarding norms pertaining to women's human rights, this section first sets forth the variety of sources of such norms and then discusses the particular status of Afghanistan's legal obligations.

Applicable International Norms

The situation of women in Afghanistan illustrates how norms generally classified as "civil and political rights" and those classified as "social, economic and cultural rights" are entirely interdependent. The enjoyment of women's "economic" right to health requires the "civil" freedoms of movement to reach health care facilities as well as information about health matters. In turn, in order to be meaningful, freedom of information requires not only the enjoyment of other "civil" rights such as expression and association in order for women to gather and disseminate knowledge about health-related issues, but also the "social" right to education in order for women to be able to assimilate information.[246] Together, the International Covenant on Civil and Political Rights (ICCPR), which emphasizes women's rights to bodily integrity, information, political participation, association, and movement and its twin, the International Covenant on Economic, Social and Cultural Rights (ICESCR), which emphasizes such substantive rights as education and health care, provide the foundation for many of the rights necessary for women to enjoy health and access to health care.[247]

The ICCPR, to which Afghanistan is a party, recognizes the right to life;[248] the right to be free from torture and cruel or inhumane treatment;[249] the right to liberty and security of person, which includes the right not to be subjected to arbitrary arrest or detention;[250] the right to freedom of movement;[251] equality before the law and rights to due process;[252] the right to be free from arbitrary or unlawful interference with his privacy, family and home;[253] the right to freedom of conscience and religion;[254] the right to freedom of expression;[255] the rights to freedom of assembly and association;[256] and the right to take part in political affairs.[257] It also guarantees the right to freely enter into marriage and have a family voluntarily.[258]

The ICESCR, to which Afghanistan is also a party, establishes, among others: the following rights relevant to women's health in Afghanistan: the right to work;[259] the right to the "highest attainable standard of physical and mental health," including "the creation of conditions which would assure to all medical service and medical attention in the event of sickness";[260] the right of everyone to education "directed to the full development of the human personality and the sense of its dignity, and shall

---

[246] Conversely, the United Nations Special Rapporteur noted "the general 'feminization of poverty' in Afghanistan as a result of women's marginalization stemming from the non-recognition of some of their basic human rights," which in turn promotes ill-health. *The Situation in Afghanistan and its Implications for International Peace and Security,* General Assembly Security Council, Report of the Secretary-General on the situation in Afghanistan. S/1997894. (November 14, 1997) at ¶ 70. [hereinafter *Situation in Afghanistan*].

[247] *International Covenant on Civil and Political Rights,* United Nations G.A. Res. 2200a (XXI), U.N. GAOR, 21st Sess., Supp. no 16., UN Doc A/6316 (1967), reprinted in Center for the Study of Human Rights, *Women and Human Rights: The Basic Documents.* New York, NY: Columbia University, (1996) [hereinafter "ICCPR"]. *International Covenant on Economic, Social and Cultural Rights,* 21 G.A. Res. 2200 (XXI), UN GAOR, Supp. (No. 16) 49, UN Doc A (6316) 1966 [hereinafter, "ICESCR"].

[248] ICCPR, Article 6.

[249] *Id,* Article 7.

[250] *Id,* Article 9.

[251] *Id,* Article 12.

[252] *Id,* Article 14.

[253] *Id,* Article 17.

[254] *Id,* Article 18.

[255] *Id,* Article 19.

[256] *Id,* Articles 21, 22.

[257] *Id,* Article 25.

[258] *Id,* Article 23.

[259] *ICESCR,* Article 7.

[260] *Id,* Article 12(d).

strengthen the respect for human rights and fundamental freedoms";[261] and the right of everyone to take part in cultural life and to enjoy the benefits of scientific progress and its applications, such as health.[262]

In recognition of economic limitations on certain States, the ICESCR requires each State Party to "take steps...to the maximum of its available resources" to achieve progressively the full realization of the rights contained in the treaty. It is a clear violation of the terms of the ICESCR, however, to take any action, through legislation or otherwise, that revokes or removes rights previously enjoyed in that state.[263] Thus, the Taliban's affirmative actions to restrict the rights previously enjoyed by women in Afghanistan, such as education, the right to work, and health care, constitute unequivocal violations of Afghanistan's obligations under the ICESCR.

Moreover, both the ICCPR and the ICESCR state in Article 1 that all of the substantive provisions contained in each of them are to be enjoyed and fulfilled on a basis of non-discrimination. The principle of non-discrimination is the cornerstone of international human rights law and is the norm against which the Taliban have committed gross violations of human rights, in both their imposition of restrictive regulations concerning women's activities and movement and their punishments for not abiding by their particular interpretation of religious practice. The Taliban's peculiar interpretation of Islam, which attempts to portray women as essentially different from men in ways that imply they have fewer rights, is simply incompatible with the core concepts of human rights. Just as any single religious interpretation cannot justify racial apartheid, neither can it be used to justify gender apartheid.[264]

The Universal Declaration of Human Rights (the "Universal Declaration"), which has come to be considered not only an authoritative interpretation of Articles 1, 55, and 56 of the UN Charter but as setting out universally agreed-upon standards and aspirations for all states, pronounces that all people are born free and equal in dignity and rights. In particular, Article 2 of the Universal Declaration states:

> *Everyone is entitled to all the rights and freedoms set forth in this Declaration, without distinction of any kind, such as race, color, sex, language, religion, political or other opinion, national or social origin, property, birth or other status.*

---

[261] *Id*, Article 13.

[262] *Id*, Article 15.

[263] *Maastricht Guidelines On Violations of Economic, Social and Cultural Rights*, Maastricht Conference, Maastricht, Holland (22-26 January 1997).

[264] See Cook, R. Reservations to the Convention on the Elimination of All Forms of Discrimination Against Women. 30 *Virginia J. of Int'l L* 643.

Thus, it is clear that non-discrimination applies both to the Taliban's discrimination against women on the grounds of their gender as well as to discrimination and punishment meted out for holding a different religious or political belief or opinion.

A panoply of international human rights documents speak to non-discrimination against women and the promotion and protection of women's health-related rights in particular. For example, the 1966 Convention on the Political Rights of Women, which Afghanistan ratified, provides for universal suffrage for women, their eligibility for election to all publicly-elected bodies and their right to hold public office.[265] The far more extensive 1979 Convention on the Elimination of All Forms of Discrimination against Women ("Women's Convention"), seems in its entirety anathema to the project of the Taliban in Afghanistan. While Afghanistan is a signatory and not a party to the Women's Convention, its signature indicates an agreement not to contravene its provisions, which include "taking all appropriate measures" to eliminate discrimination against women and to "modify social and cultural patterns of conduct... which are based on the idea of the inferiority or the superiority of either of the sexes or on stereotyped roles for men and women." [266]

The Women's Convention requires States Parties to eliminate discrimination in both public and private spheres; in education, health care, employment, economic and legal programs and rules, and all matters involving marriage and the family. Specifically, Article 10(h) of the Women's Convention addresses the right to equality in education: "Access to specific education information to help to ensure the health and well-being of families, including information and advice on family planning." Article 12 of the Women's Convention obligates States Parties to "take all appropriate measures to eliminate discrimination against women in the field of health care in order to ensure, on a basis of equality of men and women, access to health care services, including those related to family planning."[267] Article 16 addresses marriage and the family

---

[265] *Convention on the Political Rights of Women,* 193 U.N.T.S 135, (entered into force 7 July 1954), reprinted in Center for the Study of Human Rights, *Women and Human Rights: The Basic Documents,* New York, NY: Columbia University (1996). Articles 1,2,3.

[266] Article 16(a), *Convention on the Elimination of All Forms of Discrimination Against Women,* adopted 18 Dec 1979, GA Res 34/180, UN GAOR Supp (No 46), UN Doc/ A/34/36 (1978), reprinted in ILM 33 (1980)(entered into force 3 Sept. 1981)[hereinafter, "Women's Convention"].

[267] Article 12(2) continues: "Notwithstanding the provisions of paragraph I of this article, States parties shall ensure to women appropriate services in connection with pregnancy, confinement and the post-natal period, granting free services where necessary, as well as adequate nutrition during pregnancy and lactation." *Id,* Article 12(2).

and provides that States Parties shall ensure men and women have equal rights. Part (e) of Article 16 requires States Parties to ensure "[t]he same rights to decide freely and responsibly on the number and spacing of their children and to have access to the information, education and means to enable them to exercise these rights."[268] Article 2 requires States Parties to implement the substantive provisions of the Women's Convention through domestic law.[269] The Taliban's edicts, which have, among other things, eliminated education for girls, contraception and almost all access to health care are antithetical to the letter and the entire spirit of the Women's Convention and, more generally, to the universality of human rights as applying to women.

The Convention on the Rights of the Child ("CRC"), which Afghanistan has ratified, also breaks down the traditional public-private distinction and sets out a number of important provisions regarding official treatment and public rights of girl-children as well as the role of women in the private realm of the family. The CRC defines a child as anyone under 18 years of age, which makes it applicable not only to small girls but also to many young women of marrying age in Afghanistan. Many of the articles mirror provisions in the twin covenants, the ICCPR and the ICESCR. For example, the right of freedom of expression and information;[270] the right of freedom of thought, conscience and religion;[271] the right of freedom of association;[272] the right to education;[273] the right to be free from torture or other cruel, inhuman or degrading treatment or punishment;[274] and the right to the "highest attainable standard of health and health facilities," including the obligation of states parties "to ensure appropriate pre- and post-natal health care for expectant mothers". [275]Again, the Taliban's denial of health education— as well as all other education to girls— and health care, coupled with the degrading treatment meted out without due process by the Religious

---

[268] *Id*, Article 16.

[269] *Id*, Article 2.

[270] *Convention on the Rights of the Child*, G.A. Res. 44/25, 44 U.N. GAOR, Supp. No 49, U.N. Doc. A/44/736 (1989) [hereinafter, "CRC"], Article 13.

[271] *Id*, Article 14.

[272] *Id*, Article 15.

[273] *Id,* Article 31.

[274] *Id*, Article 37.

[275] *Id,* Article 24 (d) (e). The CRC also contains additional provisions unique to its subject matter regarding the equal responsibility of parents for the child's upbringing (Art. 18) and special protections for persons under 18 in the criminal justice system (Art. 40).

Police are in direct contravention of the CRC, which has achieved consensual support among more than 180 States Parties.

It is worth stressing that "cruel, inhuman or degrading treatment" has been explicitly deemed to include the punishments exacted on Afghan women with no due process by the ubiquitous Religious Police for not abiding by the Taliban's strict dress codes or for being out in public. For example, the UN Special Rapporteur for Afghanistan noted that in the past:

> *The behavior of some members of the Taliban forces, in particular in Kabul and Herat, amounted to cruel and degrading treatment and punishment. A number of women in Kabul whose veils were deemed insufficiently long were reportedly beaten on the street with chains. During his visit to Herat, the Special Rapporteur was informed that a women's arm was broken in two places for no apparent reason while she was shopping in a marketplace. He was also informed about the women who participated in the peaceful demonstration in Herat to protest against the closing of female bathhouses who were severely beaten and doused with water from a fire hose. In addition to chains and whips, people were allegedly also beaten with water hoses filled with pebbles.[276]*

Not only are these actions prohibited under the ICCPR and the CRC, but they also violate the Convention Against Torture and Other Cruel, Inhuman or Degrading Treatment ("CAT"), to which Afghanistan is a party.

In addition to these binding treaties, multiple declarations relating to women's health are relevant for their moral authority and interpretive value. Among these are the declaration and program of action from the World Conference on Human Rights ("Vienna Declaration"),[277] the Programme of Action for the International Conference on Population and Development ("Cairo Programme"),[278] and the Platform of Action of the Fourth World Conference on Women ("Beijing Platform").[279] The government of Afghanistan was represented at all of these international conferences. Taken together, these declarative documents speak to a strong

---

[276] *Question of the Violation of Human Rights and Fundamental Freedoms in any Part of the World, With Particular Reference to Colonial and Other Dependent Countries and Territories,* Economic and Social Council Distr., Commission on Human Rights. GENERAL E/CN.4/1997/59 (February 20, 1997) [hereinafter "Question of the Violation"].

[277] *Vienna Declaration and Programme of Action,* World Conference on Human Rights, Vienna. UN Doc A/Conf. 157/23 (12 July 1993).

[278] *Programme of Action of the United Nations International Conference on Population and Development.* UN Doc A/Conf. 171/13. (18 October 1994) [hereinafter, "Cairo Programme"].

[279] *Beijing Declaration and Platform for Action,* Fourth World Conference on Women. UN Doc A/Conf. 177/20 (17 October 1995) [herinafter, "Beijing Declaration"].

and growing international consensus regarding certain core principles of women's dignity, opportunities and equality with men which the Taliban's rule has flouted in every respect.

The Vienna Declaration was the first of these documentary guidelines and was issued in 1993. Part I of the Vienna Declaration states:

> *The human rights of women and of the girl-child are an inalienable, integral and indivisible part of universal human rights. The full and equal participation of women in political, civil, economic, social and cultural life, at the national, regional and international levels, and the eradication of all forms of discrimination on the grounds of sex are priority objectives of the international community.*[280]

Other relevant sections of the Vienna Declaration urge the full and equal enjoyment by women of all human rights;[281] the elimination of violence against women;[282] and the eradication of all forms of discrimination against women;[283] and establish that the equal status of women and the human rights of women should be integrated in the mainstream activity.[284]

The Cairo Programme, which emerged from the International Conference on Population and Development held in Cairo, Egypt in 1994, contains an entire chapter on gender equity and the empowerment of women . Chapter IV of that document states:

> *The empowerment and autonomy of women and the improvement of their political, social, economic and health status is a highly important end in itself. In addition, improving the status of women also enhances their decision-making capacity at all levels in all spheres of life, especially in the area of sexuality and reproduction.*[285]

In turn, the Cairo Programme calls for, among other things, eliminating inequalities between men and women that affect women's health. For example, it declares the need for State action with respect to: equal

---

[280] Part II, Section 3 deals with the equal status of and human rights of women and (40) and (41) reference health in the following way:

The World Conference on Human Rights recognized the importance of the enjoyment by women of the highest standard of physical and mental health throughout their life span and reaffirms, on the basis of equality between women and men, a woman's right to accessible and adequate health care and the widest range of family planning services, as well as equal access to education at all levels.

[281] *Vienna Declaration,* Article 36.

[282] *Id,* Article 38.

[283] *Id,* Article 39.

[284] *Id,* Article 37.

[285] *Cairo Programme,* Article 4.1.

political participation, education, skill development and employment; eliminating all practices that discriminate against women; assisting women to establish and realize their rights, including those that relate to reproductive and sexual health; improving women's ability to earn income; eliminating discriminatory practices by employers against women; and making it possible, through laws, regulations and other appropriate measures, for women to combine the roles of child-bearing, breast-feeding and child-rearing with participation in the workforce.

The Beijing Platform, which came out of the Fourth World Conference on Women in 1995, recognized "the basic right of all couples and individuals to decide freely and responsibly the number, spacing and timing of their children and have the information and means to do so, and the right to attain the highest standard of sexual and reproductive health."

Other relevant references in the Beijing Declaration refer to Equal rights for men and women;[286] measures governments should take to promote women's rights;[287] the inalienability of women's human rights;[288] the equal enjoyment by women of economic, social and cultural rights;[289] the need to eliminate violence against women, including that based on cultural prejudices;[290] the need to eliminate discrimination based on race, language, ethnicity, culture, religion, disability, or socioeconomic class;[291] and the value of human rights education.[292]

Section 76, which deals with gender-biased curricula and teaching materials, specifically mentions reproductive health when it states: "The lack of sexual and reproductive health education has a profound impact on women and men." Strategic objectives in the Beijing Platform include the eradication of illiteracy among women; the improvement of women's access to vocational training, science and technology, and continuing education and the development of non-discriminatory education and training. Needless to say, the Taliban's programs are entirely contrary to the Beijing Platform, as well as the other two declarative instruments.

Given the Taliban's invocation of Islam to justify their restriction and violation of women's rights, another declaration of particular relevance for Afghanistan is the Cairo Declaration on Human Rights in Islam

---

[286] *Beijing Declaration,* Chapter IV, ¶ 214.

[287] *Id,* ¶ 215.

[288] *Id,* ¶ 216.

[289] *Id,* ¶ 220.

[290] *Id,* ¶ 224.

[291] *Id,* ¶ 225.

[292] *Id,* ¶. 227.

("Cairo Declaration"), which was signed by the Organization of the Islamic Conference in 1990.[293] Afghanistan is currently one of the 55 members of the Organization of the Islamic Conference, the charter of which states as two of its principal objectives: the elimination of discrimination and the "support of international peace and security founded on justice."[294] Article 7 of the Cairo Declaration, states: "As of the moment of birth, every child has rights due from the parents, society and the state to be accorded proper nursing, education and material, hygienic and moral care. Both the fetus and the mother must be protected and accorded special care."[295] With respect to girls' education, Article 7(b) states: "Parents and those in such like capacity have the right to choose the type of education they desire for their children, provided they take into consideration the interest and future of the children in accordance with ethical values and the principles of the *Shari'a*."[296] Implicit in this provision is that families ought to be able to provide education to all children, including girl children. Furthermore, Article 9 of the Cairo Declaration explicitly provides that education is to be provided for all children, including girl children.[297] The Cairo Declaration is filled with other provisions that explicitly contradict the actions the Taliban has taken under the justification of the *Shari'a*. For example, it specifies: the right to safety from bodily harm;[298] women's right to equality with men;[299] the right to free movement and place of residence;[300] the right to enjoy scientific, literary, artistic or technical production, including that relating to health;[301] and the right to equality before the law.[302]

---

[293] *The Cairo Declaration on Human Rights in Islam,* (signed by Organization of the Islamic Conference on 5 August 1990), reprinted in Center for the Study of Human Rights. *Twenty-Five Human Rights Documents.* New York, NY: Columbia University, 1994. [herinafter, "Cairo Declaration"].

[294] Organization of the Islamic Conference, in *International Organizations: The Middle East and North Africa 1996.* London: Europa Publications Limited, 1995. p. 231.

[295] Cairo Declaration, Article 7.

[296] *Id*, Article 7(b).

[297] *Id*, Article 9.

[298] *Id.,* Article 2 (d).

[299] *Id*, Article 6.

[300] *Id*, Article 12.

[301] *Id*, Article 16.

[302] *Id*, Article 19.

Status of Afghanistan's International Legal Obligations

Under international law the Taliban is responsible for adherence to human rights law Afghanistan has ratified, notwithstanding the fact that its leadership does not recognize the validity of these to the extent that they depart from the Taliban's particular interpretation of *Shari'a*. Moreover, that the Taliban does not possess all of the attributes of a functioning and recognized government does not relieve it of accountability for the human rights violations it has committed.

Under previous governments, Afghanistan became a party to a large number of human rights treaties without substantive reservations. For example, Afghanistan was among the first countries to accede to the Convention on the Political Rights of Women in 1966. Afghanistan acceded to the ICCPR and the ICESCR on January 24, 1983 without reservations.[303] It ratified the CAT on April 1, 1987. As noted above, Afghanistan has even signed—although is not a party to— the Women's Convention.[304]

After the expulsion of Soviet-backed regime in 1992, the *mujaheddin* groups in power in Afghanistan and subsequently the Taliban adopted a different attitude toward human rights treaties. On the one hand, Afghanistan ratified the CRC on March 28, 1994, which, as noted above, contains many provisions affecting women, the organization of the family and girl-children. However, in so doing it made a general reservation to the effect that: "the Government of the Republic of Afghanistan reserves the right to express, upon ratifying the Convention, reservations on all provisions of the Convention that are incompatible with the laws of Islamic *Shari'a* and the local legislation in effect."[305]

Declarations and reservations based on religious objection must generally be respected; however, local customs and legislation cannot be

---

[203] Some treaties place conditions upon which States may become Parties through ratification. Under international law, accession equally indicates the consent of a given State to be bound by the provisions of the treaty. See *Vienna Convention on the Law of Treaties*, 1155 U.N.T.S. 331 (23 May, 1969), Articles 11, 12, 14(1), [hereinafter, "Vienna Convention"]. Note also Afghanistan's declarations upon accession objecting to the limitation of States Parties to the ICCPR and ICESCR.

[304] Afghanistan signed the Women's Convention on August 14, 1980.

[305] A reservation is a unilateral statement by a ratifying state which "purports to exclude or to modify the legal effect of certain provisions of the treaty in their application to that state." A "declaration" in contrast specifies the state's understanding or interpretation of a given provision or set of provisions in the treaty. The Although nominally a "declaration," Afghanistan's "declaration" attempts to amend the CRC *pro tanto*, in order to change future obligations among itself and the other parties and is therefore treated as a reservation by the United Nations. See *Vienna Convention*, Article 2(d).

used as an excuse for failing to attempt compliance with the treaty.[306] That is, under international law, reservations—whether based on religion or any other objection— must be narrowly tailored, rather than sweeping justifications for abdication. Article 51(2) of the CRC specifically prohibits reservations that are "incompatible with the object and purpose of the treaty;" under the terms of the CRC as well as international law generally, such reservations are not permissible and not given legal effect.[307] Broadly-worded reservations that attempt to excuse the Taliban from responsibility for upholding fundamental human rights principles, such as non-discrimination, as well as specific obligations central to the promotion of children's well-being and development, such as to health care and education, are clearly contrary to the object and purpose of the CRC.

It is important to note that the *Shari'a* is not one single law, but rather is derived from multiple sources. As discussed below, "[d]ifferent and often conflicting laws make up the totality of what is collectively known as the *Shari'a*."[308] Indeed, the *Shari'a* is often cited as expounding the fundamental equality among races and between the sexes. For example, the Committee on the Elimination of Discrimination Against Women (CEDAW), which is charged with the monitoring the Women's Convention, has specifically stated in observations that "[t]he Shariah itself gave equality to women, but the problem that had to be overcome was that of interpretation."[309] CEDAW has urged governments to undertake efforts "to proceed to an interpretation of the Shariah that was permissible and did not block the advancement of women."[310] CEDAW has forcefully declared that reservations based on the *Shari'a* "that were not compatible with the goals of the [Women's] Convention were not acceptable."[311]

While the CRC was ratified by the government of President Burhanuddin Rabbani, the Taliban rejects the validity of not only treaty-

---

[306] See Venkatraman, BA. Islamic States and the United Nations Convention on the Elimination of All Forms of Discrimination Against Women: Are the *Shari'a* and the Convention Compatible?, 44 *Am. U. L. Rev.* 1949, 2008 (1995).

[307] *Id.*

[308] Venkatramen, S*upra,* 61, p. 1964.

[309] *Report of the Committee on the Elimination of Discrimination Against Women*, Thirteenth session, UN General Assembly, Forty-Ninth session, supp. No. 38, (1994), at ¶132.

[310] *Id,* ¶ 132.

[311] *Id.*

but also Charter-based international human rights obligations.[312] In so doing, the Taliban employs two often inconsistent arguments: incompatibility with the *Shari'a*; and inability to perform.[313] Neither is valid.

First, Mr. Choong-Hyun Paik, the UN Special Rapporteur for Afghanistan reports that in meetings with the Taliban-designated Attorney General, this official "indicated that if a promise, convention, treaty or other instrument, even if it was in the Charter of the United Nations, was contrary to *Shari'a,* they would not fulfil it or act on it"[314]:

> *We accept Shari'a, our God's convention . . . . If someone is drinking in public, even if the Covenant or the United Nations Charter says they should not be punished, we will. The core of our action and our policy is the law of God, as contained in the Qur'an. We do not follow individuals, or people of other countries. We follow the law of God. We adhere strictly to what the Qur'an is telling us. Therefore, we invite all people in the world to follow the Qur'an. Any laws that negate the Qur'an or the law of God, we don't accept that.[315]*

The Special Rapporteur's report also notes that the Taliban authorities indicated that although they were willing to accept human rights conventions, "the concept and meaning of human rights were totally dependent on God's will."[316] The Governor of Kabul told the UN Special Rapporteur that "the provisions of international human rights instruments could not be applied if they conflicted with God's law. [Our] domestic interpretation of human rights [is] not based on individual rights."[317]

As stated above, the Taliban is not free to disregard all international law that is not in accordance with their particular interpretation of *Shari'a.* It is a fundamental tenet of modern international human rights law that certain principles that govern the way a state or quasi-state may treat its subjects transcend domestic legislation and customs. This principle, which allowed for judgment of the crimes against humanity committed in Nazi Germany and ultimately prevailed in the dismantling of racial apartheid in South Africa, applies equally to the situation of gender apartheid in Afghanistan under the Taliban.

---

[312] Charter-based obligations are assumed by virtue of being members in the United Nations.

[313] While certain public statements issued by the Taliban appear to question the authority and legitimacy of the Soviet-backed regime to undertake international obligations, it has not pressed this argument with the United Nations.

[314] *Question of the Violation.,* ¶ 31.

[315] *Id.*

[316] *Id,* ¶ 33.

[317] *Id.*

Second, at times, the Taliban does not base its non-compliance on religious grounds at all, but rather claims "impossibility of performance" with respect to its human rights obligations, arguing that they are waiting to achieve political stability before the Taliban can establish the conditions for women's basic rights, such as education and employment.[318] For example, the Special Rapporteur's 1997 report notes:

> *The most frequent responses by representatives of the Taliban authorities regarding the resumption of female employment and education have been: "we are in an emergency situation", "when security conditions are restored", "we are in a situation of war and want to restore peace and a centralized government", "until there is peace and stability", the latest one being "when we are in control".[319]*

Not only, as the Special Rapporteur notes, does this appear "to be at odds with the affirmation of most officials that peace and security have been brought to all areas under their control,"[320] but it also underlines the political nature of the Taliban's claims—at times invoking religion and tradition and at times justifying their conduct on the grounds of incapacity.

Moreover, it is important to keep clearly in mind that neither the nonderogable rights under the ICCPR nor some provisions of international humanitarian law relating to the treatment of civilians during armed conflict can be suspended during emergency or wartime. Article 4(2) of the ICCPR expressly states: "No derogation from articles 6, 7, 8 (paragraphs 1 and 2), 11, 15, 16 and 18 may be made under this provision." Among the most relevant for purposes of Afghanistan are that Article 6 specifies the right to life; Article 7 prohibits torture or cruel, inhuman or degrading treatment; Article 15 prohibits *ex post facto* punishment; Article 16 recognizes the right of everyone to be recognized as a person before the law; and, perhaps most pertinent, Article 18 establishes freedom of thought, conscience and religion.[321] Specifically, Article 18 provides: "This right shall include freedom to have or to adopt a religion or belief

---

[318] That is, under international law, the fact that the government of Afghanistan has changed since accession or signature of these treaties does not terminate or suspend the State's treaty obligations, even if States Parties to the treaty have suspended diplomatic relations and do not recognize the Taliban as the legitimate government of Afghanistan. Only a fundamental change in circumstances justifies the termination of or withdrawal from a treaty only under circumstances of impossibility of performance (*rebus sic standibus*). See *Vienna Convention,* Articles 54, 57.61(2).

[319] *Question of the Violation,,* ¶114.

[320] *Id.*

[321] Article 8(1)-(2) prohibits slavery and servitude; Article 11 prohibits imprisonment for contractual breach.

of his choice, and freedom, either individually or in community with others and in public or private, to manifest his religion or belief in worship, observance, practice and teaching." In direct opposition to the Taliban's monolithic edicts and enforcement of religious doctrine, Article 18 specifies: "No one shall be subject to coercion which would impair his freedom to have to adopt a religion or belief of his choice." That is, international human rights law is fundamentally concerned with the free exercise of religion, including the right to reject religious doctrine, which cannot be abridged or denied on the basis of the Taliban's particular view of Islamic law.[322]

The Geneva Conventions of 1949, which Afghanistan has signed and which were often invoked by the various groups fighting the Soviet-backed regime during the 1980's and early 1990's, form the basis of modern international humanitarian law, a body of law often considered to be the international human rights law that applies during times of armed conflict. While the human rights violations specifically against women committed by the Taliban transcend the circumstances of armed conflict, it is worth noting the provisions in international humanitarian law relating to the basic guarantees that must be afforded to the civilian population by an armed group. Indeed, in many respects the Taliban is widely perceived as an alien, occupying force in cosmopolitan areas such as Kabul, where women were formerly fully engaged in economic, social and cultural activities.

Common Article 3 of the Geneva Conventions, which applies to non-international armed conflicts, requires that parties to the armed conflict accord humane treatment "without any distinction founded on race, colour, religion or faith, sex, birth or wealth, or any similar criteria" to all persons taking no active part in the hostilities including, among others, those placed in the midst of combat by sickness, wounds, or any other cause. This aspect of Common Article 3, which has come to be recognized in certain respects as customary international law that is binding upon all States, is being grossly violated by the Taliban's restrictions on women. For example, in 1997 the Special Rapporteur reported with respect to the prohibition on female doctors and health care workers and limitations on women's movement that "Taliban gender restrictions continued to interfere with the delivery of humanitarian assistance to women and girls."[323] Among other things, Common Article 3 also specifically prohibits: "violence to life and person," including cruel treatment and torture; "outrages

---

[322] This right is entirely consistent with the *Qur'an*, an oft-quoted verse of which states: "Let there be no coercion in matters of faith." Surah 2:Al-Barqarah: 256, *The Message of the Qur'an*, Muhammed Asad trans. (Gibraltar, 1980) at p. 343.

[323] *Country Report on Human Rights, Supra*, 3

upon personal dignity, in particular humiliating and degrading treatment;" and "the passing of sentences and carrying out of executions" without a trial that afforded the accused due process of law.[324] In short, Common Article 3 reinforces the basic guarantees of many of the non-derogable rights provided under the ICCPR and international human rights law.

Finally, it is worth underscoring that even though the Taliban is not an officially recognized government of Afghanistan with control over the entire territory of the country, it is still accountable for the human rights violations it has perpetrated against Afghan women.[325] On October 11,1996 the Taliban requested the seat held in the General Assembly by the Government of President Burhanuddin Rabbani, but its petition was rejected by the United Nations Credentials Committee.[326] Indeed, official recognition and credentials have been withheld due in large measure to the ever-changing military situation, but also in part to human rights concerns relating to the Taliban's treatment of women.[327]

At the United Nations, a Special Rapporteur was first appointed to examine the human rights situation in Afghanistan in 1984 by the Chairman of the Commission on Human Rights, who had been requested to do so by the Economic and Social Council. Since then, the mandate has been renewed regularly by resolutions of the Commission on Human Rights and has been endorsed by the Economic and Social Council. The Special Rapporteur submits regular reports to the Human Rights Commission and to the General Assembly of the United Nations.[328] In addition to the Commission on

---

[324] *The Geneva Conventions of August 12, 1949*, International Committee of the Red Cross, Common Article III.

[325] The Taliban has only been recognized as the official government by Pakistan, Saudi Arabia and the United Arab Emirates.

[326] *Question of the Violation.*

[327] For example, the United States has opposed recognition of the Taliban on such grounds. Assistant US Secretary of State for South Asian Affairs, Karl F. Inderfurth, stated in testimony before the Senate Foreign Relations Committee's Subcommittee on Asia and the Pacific on October 22, 1997: "...today's tightened rules on women's right to work and girls' right to education have made their situation far worse, and justifiably have shocked the world. We call upon the Taliban to lift its restrictions on the employment of women and the schooling of girls; we also call upon the Taliban and all factions to abide by internationally-accepted norms of human rights."United States Department of State, *United States Government Support for Women of Afghanistan* (January 26, 1998).

[328] See E/CN.4/1985/21, E/CN.4/1986/24, E/CN.4/1987/22, E/CN.4/1988/25, E/CN.4/1989/24, E/CN.4/1990/25, E/CN.4/1991/31, E/CN.4/1992/33, E/CN.4/1993/42, E/CN.4/1994/53, E/CN.4/1995/64, E/CN.4/1996/64, E/CN.4/1997/59 and the latter in the annexes to documents A/40/843, A/41/778, A/42/667 and Corr.1, A/43/742, A/44/669, A/45/664, A/46/606, A/47/656, A/48/584, A/49/650, A/50/567 and A/51/481. *Human Rights Questions: Human Rights Situations and Reports of Special Rapporteurs and Representatives,* UN General Assembly. A/52/493. (October 16, 1997).

Human Rights, the Economic and Social Council, the General Assembly, and the Security Council, together with committees charged with monitoring the specific treaties to which Afghanistan is a party all monitor and report on the human rights abuses committed by the Taliban.

In addition, as Afghanistan produces the largest number of refugees in the world, international standards for granting refugees status are also relevant in assessing the Taliban's responsibility for human rights violations. That is, under international law a woman becomes a refugee, and is thereby entitled to various protections from her host country, if "owing to a well-founded fear of being persecuted for reasons of race, religion, nationality, membership in a particular social group or political opinion, is outside the country of [her] nationality and is unable, or owing to such fear, unwilling to avail [herself] of the protection of that country or... unwilling to return to it."[329] "Persecution" on the grounds of political opinion and membership in a social group has been held to apply to violations of women's rights as a result of extremist interpretations of Islam with which the women do not agree. The test that is applied is not whether the perpetrator of persecution is a recognized regime but whether it exercises sufficient control over a particular area so as to preclude the person from availing herself of protection from the authorities or, alternatively, seeking remedies for violations. The Taliban's control over more than two thirds of Afghanistan's territory coupled with their domination of "government" ministries of health, justice, education and other sectors effectively precludes Afghan women of receiving protection or redress from their violations.

In short, the Taliban is bound by international human rights obligations. While freedom of religion allows for specific interpretations of and reservations under international law, it does not permit the Taliban to take measures that directly contravene the object and purpose of treaties under which it has assumed obligations nor to decline to uphold universally recognized principles of non-discrimination in the name of the *Shari'a*. Moreover, the Taliban's invocation of both religious grounds and incapacity reveal the political reality behind their non-compliance with international human rights obligations. Finally, the Taliban is responsible for protection and fulfilling the human rights of all of the subjects who inhabit the territory under its functional control.

---

[329] *Protocol Relating to the Status of Refugees of 31 January 1967*, UN Treaty Series No. 8791, Vol 606, p.267 (entered into force 4 October 1967), Article 1. The Convention was limited to Europe between 1941 and 1945. The 1967 Protocol adopted all of the substantive provisions of the Convention and omitted the temporal and geographic limitations.

VI. ISLAM AND WOMEN'S HUMAN RIGHTS

It is important to step beyond the frame of formal human rights law and to examine the Taliban's claim of divine sanction itself. Indeed, to leave such an assertion standing without the slightest question or challenge does its own kind of injustice to the women of Afghanistan. The uncritical acceptance of Taliban claims to Islamic purity and divine right grants the Taliban a level of Islamic authenticity that even their allies within the ranks of Muslim political-religious movements deny them.[330] Moreover, the failure to even question, much less dispute, the Taliban's assertions in this regard, puts the defense of women entirely outside a key frame of reference—Islam—that they rightfully claim for themselves. The finding from the PHR health and human rights survey that more than 95% of Afghan women not only disagreed with Taliban orders, but believed that such orders do not represent the requirements or teachings of Islam, makes a profoundly important statement that should not be lost.

The routine description of Taliban policies as simply "Islamic" or as a "strict interpretation" of Islam—without more—masks a far more complicated reality about the interpretation of religious texts, their articulation with local cultural practices, and the manipulation of the resulting decrees in the struggle to assert and maintain political power. Indeed, even a fairly cursory examination of the decrees and the context surrounding their imposition reveals that, despite repeated reference to *Shari'a*, or Islamic law, the prohibitions at issue here represent not the immutable word of God, but the political choices made by the Taliban in its efforts to consolidate its hold on Afghan society.

In addressing the Taliban's efforts to silence its critics by raising the mantle of respect for religion and culture,[331] it is first important to recog-

---

[330] The leaders of two of Pakistan's most conservative political-religious organizations, the *Jamiat-e Ulema-i Islam* ("the alleged patron of the Taliban") and the *Jamaat-e Islami*, have publicly criticized the Taliban for their restrictions on women. Nancy Hatch Dupree, "Afghan Women Under the Taliban," in W. Maley, ed. *Fundamentalism Reborn?: Afghanistan and the Taliban,Supra,*43 citing Pakistani newspaper reports, *The Nation* 19 October 1996 and *The Frontier Post*, 9 October 1996. See also Amnesty International, *Afghanistan: Grave abuses in the name of religion.* November 1996 at p.5.

[331] For example, in an interview with Voice of America, the head of the Taliban, Mullah Muhammed Omar, rejected criticism from Amnesty International, stating "'We are just implementing the divine injunctions.'" (www.pakistanlink.com, May 25, 1998).

nize that there is no one authoritative interpretation of Islam, nor is there a single clerical body, akin to the Vatican in Roman Catholicism, that has the acknowledged right to promulgate rules of law binding on all Muslims. Rather, the vast array of laws and practices which are understood by Muslims in different parts of the world to be *Shari'a* have emerged historically in the dramatically different settings of Asia, Africa, the Middle East and Europe where Islam spread in the first centuries after the death of the Prophet Muhammad. Throughout that history, there were political divisions and doctrinal disputes, most importantly the split between the Sunni and Shi'a sects following conflicts over the leadership of the early Muslim community after the death of the Prophet. But even within these broad divisions there exist myriad sects, schools of thought, mystical traditions, and schools of law.

Thus, *Shari'a* is not one unchanging, uncontested body of specific rules and laws. Even the description of some interpretations as "strict" and others as "liberal" implies a unity of underlying doctrine and a clear hierarchy of authenticity or purity that dangerously misrepresents the nature of diversity within Muslim societies today. In fact, *Shari'a,* though derived from the *Qur'an*, the holy book of Islam which Muslim believers consider to be the result of divine revelation,[332] and the *Sunna*, the practice or example of the Prophet as he lived his life,[333] is the result of many centuries of elaborate jurisprudential development. Even the first fairly comprehensive compilations of *Shari'a* by different jurists and their followers were not completed until the third century after the death of the Prophet.[334]

Like any sophisticated system of law, *Shari'a* includes a range of different interpretive principles and techniques that enable its adherents to adapt general principles to the exigencies of particular situations. Moreover, despite the aphorism found in many primers of Islamic law that

---

[332] The *Qur'an* provides primarily statements of general principles and standards of behavior, not detailed and precise rules of law. As one commentator explained, "the *Qur'an* is not and does not profess to be a code of law or even a law book. . . Rather, it is an eloquent appeal to mankind to obey the law of God which, it is (in the main) implied, has already been revealed or is capable of being discovered." Vesey-Fitzgerald, "Nature and Sources of the Shari'a" in Khadduri and Liebesny, eds. *Law in the Middle East* p. 87 as quoted in Abdullahi An-Na'im, *Toward an Islamic Reformation.* Syracuse University Press, 1990.

[333] The Sunna was recorded over the course of several centuries in the form of *ahadith*, or sayings, about the Prophet's life, actions or examples. There are vast numbers of *hadith*, some deemed to be more authoritative than others; and there exists a generally agreed set of principles for determining the strength of (sometimes conflicting) *hadith*.

[334] For a concise explanation of the sources and development of *Shari'a*, see Abdullahi An-Na'im, *Toward an Islamic Reformation.* Syracuse University Press, 1990.

Shari'a is a "complete code of life," the reality is that the lives of Muslims everywhere are shaped not only by human interpretations of divinely inspired law, but also by culture, by spiritual inclination and, indeed, by a significant amount of personal choice in matters of religious life.[335] This is no less true in Afghanistan with its ethnically, culturally, and religiously diverse population, than elsewhere in the Muslim world.

The precise rules promulgated via the Taliban decrees at issue here are not the words of divine revelation found in the *Qur'an*. They are the interpretations of a small group of clerics raised in the Sunni Hanafi tradition as filtered through the customary practices of rural Pashtun society. As the Special Rapporteur recently stated, "the Taliban have a highly idiosyncratic vision of Islam that has been disputed by numerous Sunni Islamic scholars as representing at best a tribal rural code of behaviour applied only in some parts of Afghanistan of which only one aspect is being exploited."[336]

Indeed, contrary to the Taliban stances on these issues, there is strong authority within Islamic law and traditions for affirmatively promoting the education of both girls and boys; for the right of women to work, own property, earn a living, and participate in public life; and for the importance of enabling women to take the steps necessary to protect and promote their own health and that of their families.[337]

As discussed above, at times the Taliban implicitly concede as much when its leaders make arguments about the feasibility of complying with international human rights obligations. Meeting with officials from the UN Department of Humanitarian Affairs in the Spring of 1997, Taliban officials reportedly "admitted... that this particular decree [closing schools for girls] was extra-Islamic but considered it justifiable under the circumstances." [338, 339] Similarly, when women were summarily expelled

---

[335] Richard W. Bulliet, "The Individual in Islamic Society," in Bloom, Martin and Proudfoot, eds. *Religious Diversity and Human Rights*. New York: Columbia University Press, 1996.

[336] *Human Rights Questions* ¶29. See also ¶137.

[337] These principles are widely accepted and practiced in Muslim countries following a range of traditions and schools of Islamic law, including the *Sunni Hanafi* school supposedly followed by the Taliban. In recent years, Islamic scholars have convened meetings and issued statements and declarations upholding these principles. *The Cairo Declaration*; *Final Report of the International Conference on Population and Reproductive Health in the Muslim World* (21-24 February 1998, Al-Azhar University , Cairo); *Health Promotion through Islamic Lifestyles: The Amman Declaration* (WHO, 1996).

[338] *DHA Report, Supra*, 1, at 2.1

[339] Significantly, the high value which the *Qur'an* place on the pursuit of learning can be seen in its directeve that education continue even in times of war. (Surah 9: *At-Tawbah*:122). See Riffat Hassan, "Rights of Women Within Islamic Communities," in J. Witte and J. van der Vyver, eds. *Religious Human Rights in Global Perspective*. (Netherlands: Martinus Nuhoff Publishers (Kluwer Law International) 1996).

from workplaces and banned from employment, Taliban authorities announced that women would be readmitted to workplaces when security conditions had improved and "Islamic conditions" had been instituted.[340] According to the Special Rapporteur, "a number of Taliban officials have stated that, in principle, the movement was not against the education and employment of women 'in honour and dignity,' a right accorded them in Islam."[341]

As noted above these arguments no more justify the Taliban's failures to comply with international human rights norms than do their blanket invocations of Islam. Indeed, the Special Rapporteur has recently listed them as "the by now customary implausible excuses" for failing to re-establish women's access to education, employment and health care: "'when peace and security is achieved,' 'when there are sufficient funds for implementing segregated education,' 'when we take over the entire country,' 'there will be protests in other parts of the country if we allow it here.'"[342] As the Special Rapporteur has pointed out, these excuses stand in direct contradiction to the Taliban's claim that among its primary accomplishments has been the restoration of security for the population, including women, in the areas they control.

Under these circumstances, it is deeply unfair to the people of Afghanistan to pose the issue as one of Islam versus human rights. It is not the divine dictates of Islam, but rather the decidedly earthly strategic decisions of the Taliban to put military advantage, social control and personal power above the well-being of women, that should be judged by the standards of universal human rights.

---

[340] *Question of the Violation* ¶¶ 69-70.

[341] Id at ¶ 80.

[342] *Human Rights Questions* ¶¶ 75, 98.

[343] See Chapter II.

VII. RECOMMENDATIONS

To the Taliban:
- The Taliban must commit themselves to take all measures necessary to stop the practice of systematic discrimination against women and guarantee women's human rights.
- Taliban officials must respect rights to due process as required by international human rights instruments under which it has assumed obligations. Those who breach rights to due process should be held criminally responsible and prosecuted in accordance with international human rights standards.
- All law enforcement and security personnel should be ordered to respect human rights and should receive adequate training in human rights standards, including women's human rights, prevention of violations, and prisoners' rights.
- Security personnel and others responsible for these abuses should be held criminally responsible and prosecuted in accordance with international human rights standards. Victims of abuse should receive fair and adequate compensation, including the means for as full rehabilitation as possible.

To the International Community:
- The international community must not accept any justifications for systematic discrimination against Afghan women. Representation of Afghanistan at the United Nations should not be afforded to any party whose policies, either explicit or implicit, discriminate against women.
- The international community should also consider ways in which those responsible for the vast degradation of women and girls in Afghanistan might be held accountable before the world for these human rights violations. The United Nations Human Rights Commission should call a special session for purposes of creating a Commission of Experts to investigate the systematic and egregious human rights violations against women in Afghanistan and to create measures to hold those responsible accountable.
- International human rights monitors should be deployed to collect and publicly disseminate information on rights abuses, especially those against women, by all parties and from all parts of the country.

- The UN's Memorandum of Understanding with the Taliban should be rescinded and re-negotiated. If the UN fails to reach an agreement that would assure the immediate access of Afghan women and girls to health care and education and an end to restrictions on the operations of humanitarian organizations (including limits on the movement of their Muslim female staff), then it should publicly announce that it is terminating negotiations with the Taliban, restricting its aid to humanitarian operations carried out by non-governmental organizations, and removing UN staff from Afghanistan to the maximum extent feasible.

To Health and Humanitarian Assistance Providers:
- Humanitarian intervention programs should reevaluate aid distribution procedures to ensure that those most in need are not discriminated against. One way to accomplish this would be for agencies to develop impact assessments regarding human rights, especially women's human rights, which they should factor into their policy decisions and field procedures. In particular, the system of distributing assistance through local political leaders (*wakeels*) should be reviewed, as there is evidence to suggest that these individuals, in many cases, are not distributing the assistance to those most in need.
- Providers of humanitarian assistance in Afghanistan have been all but shut down by the Taliban, which has increasingly interfered with their operations, by closing down private schools for girls, prohibiting women from directly receiving humanitarian aid, and by ordering relief workers out of the city and into inhabitable barracks on Kabul's outskirts. As a consequence, almost all relief providers left Kabul in late July. This vacuum will almost certainly result in enormous added privation, especially for women and girls. PHR urges those providers who remain in Afghanistan to protest restrictions and discrimination and redouble their efforts to overcome these in their administration of humanitarian assistance.
- At such time as humanitarian aid workers are permitted to resume operations in Afghanistan, PHR urges them to reevaluate aid distribution procedures to assure that women and children receive the bulk of food aid. To the maximum extent feasible, health and humanitarian assistance providers must insist that distribution of aid and access to programs be carried out in a non-discriminatory manner. They must make every effort to overcome the barriers to women's receipt of assistance.
- The extent of mental health problems identified in this study indicates an urgent need for humanitarian organizations to provide mental health services for women.
- Afghan women who seek refuge outside of Afghanistan should be officially recognized as refugees by the United Nations High Commissioner for Refugees (UNHCR) and afforded assistance accordingly.

- Finally, international donors should continue their humanitarian assistance to refugees in Pakistan and Iran and ensure that their aid is distributed without discrimination. They should pay close attention to the needs of newly arriving refugees in Pakistan, who appear to be wholly underserved and are in need of shelter, food, and health services.

To Multinational Corporations:

- Corporate investment in Afghanistan directly and indirectly aids the Taliban regime, and contributes to the suffering of the Afghan people, especially women. For this reason, PHR calls for a moratorium on investment in Afghanistan, including the oil and gas pipelines proposed by a consortium of multinational corporations, including UNOCAL, based in California and Bridas of Argentina.[343]

    Such a moratorium should remain in place until women are guaranteed their human rights.

To the United States Government:

- The United States should follow through on Secretary Albright's demand that the Taliban protect and promote the human rights of women in Afghanistan. The United States should take every opportunity to condemn the Taliban's oppression of women in international fora and to demand that the Taliban adhere to the requirements of international law.
- The United States should make plain that it does not and will not recognize any government that systematically disenfranchises women. It should continue to oppose a claim by the Taliban for a seat at the United Nations as the government of Afghanistan.
- The United States should continue to maintain a leading role in peace negotiations between Taliban and anti-Taliban forces. These negotiations must include provisions to end the systematic discrimination of women in Afghanistan. "Peace" will come to Afghanistan only when women's human rights are protected and promoted in Afghanistan.
- The United States should call upon the government of Pakistan and other governments that support the Taliban to end that support.
- The United States should do all that is possible to include the protection and promotion of women's human rights in humanitarian assistance policies. It should denounce restrictions on humanitarian aid imposed by the Taliban and urge nations and NGOs providing aid to find ways of circumventing these restrictions.
- The United States should work with UN officials and other countries to designate Afghan women who flee gender-based persecution by the Taliban as refugees.

---

[343] See Chapter II.

APPENDIX A

NOTE: The following document is an appendix to the *Final report on the situation of human rights in Afghanistan,* GENERAL E/CN.4/1997/59 (February 20, 1997), submitted by Mr. Choong Hyun Paik, Special Rapporteur, in accordance with Commission on Human Rights resolution 1996/75, as it appears in the web site: www.reliefweb.int

Economic and Social Council Distr. GENERAL E/CN.4/1997/59
20 February 1997 Original: ENGLISH

COMMISSION ON HUMAN RIGHTS
Fifty-third session
Item 10 of the provisional agenda
Question of the Violation of Human Rights and Fundamental Freedoms In Any Part of the World, with Particular Reference to Colonial and Other Dependent Countries and Territories

Final report on the situation of human rights in Afghanistan submitted by Mr. Choong-Hyun Paik, Special Rapporteur, in accordance with Commission on Human Rights resolution 1996/75

Notice of Department for enforcement of right Islamic way and prevention of evils:

The Department for enforcement of right Islamic way and prevention of evils for the implementation of legal Islamic orders and prophet Mohamad tradition in order to prevent evils which cause serious dangers and problems for Islamic society requests from all pious sisters and brothers to seriously follow 8 articles mentioned below to prevent occurrence of evils:

1. No exit and traveling of sisters without escort of legal close relative (Mahram).
2. Those sisters are coming out of their homes with legal escort should use veil (burqa) or similar things to cover the face.
3. Sitting of sisters in the front seat of cart (gadi) and Jeep (vehicle) without legal relative is forbidden. In the case of appearance serious measures will be carried out against the vehicle and cart rider/driver.

4. Shopkeepers do not have right to buy or sell things with those women without covered face, otherwise the shopkeeper is guilty and has no right to complain.
5. Cars are strictly forbidden to be covered with flowers for wedding ceremony and also is not allowed to drive around the city.
6. Women's invitations in hotels and wedding party in hotels are forbidden.
7. Sisters without legal close relative with them can not use taxis, otherwise the taxi driver is responsible.
8. The person who is in charge of collecting fares (money) for sisters in buses, minibuses and jeeps should be under 10 years old.

The professional delegates of this department are in charge to punish violators according to Islamic principles.

APPENDIX B

NOTE: The following document is an appendix to the *Final report on the situation of human rights in Afghanistan,* GENERAL E/CN.4/1997/59 (February 20, 1997), submitted by Mr. Choong Hyun Paik, Special Rapporteur, in accordance with Commission on Human Rights resolution 1996/75, as it appears in the web site: www.reliefweb.int

Economic and Social Council Distr. GENERAL E/CN.4/1997/59
20 February 1997 Original: ENGLISH

COMMISSION ON HUMAN RIGHTS
Fifty-third session
Item 10 of the provisional agenda
Question of the Violation of Human Rights and Fundamental Freedoms In Any Part of the World, with Particular Reference to Colonial and Other Dependent Countries and Territories

Final report on the situation of human rights in Afghanistan submitted by Mr. Choong-Hyun Paik, Special Rapporteur, in accordance with Commission on Human Rights resolution 1996/75

(Translation of Order)
Taliban Islamic Movement of Afghanistan Rules of work for the State hospitals and private clinics based on *Shari'a* principles

1. Female patients should go to female physicians. In case a male physician is needed, the female patient should be accompanied by her close relatives (*mahram*).
2. During examination, the female patients and male physicians both should be dressed with Islamic *Hijab*.
3. Male physicians should not touch or see the other parts of female patients except the affected part.
4. Waiting rooms for female patients should be safely covered.

---

[343] See Chapter II.

5. The person who regulates turns for female patients should be a female.
6. During night duty, in the rooms where female patients are hospitalized, a male doctor without the call of patient is not allowed to enter the room.
7. Sitting and speaking between male and female doctors are not allowed. If there be need for discussion, it should be done with *hejab*.
8. Female doctors should wear simple clothes, they are not allowed to wear stylish clothes or use cosmetics and makeup.
9. Female doctors and nurses are not allowed to enter the rooms where male patients are hospitalized.
10. Hospital staff should pray in the mosque on time. The director of hospital is bound to assign a place and appoint a priest (*mullah*) for prayer.
11. Staff of (Amri Bel Maroof Wa Nai Az Munkar) Department are allowed to go for control at any time and nobody can prevent them. Anybody who violates the order will be punished as per Islamic regulations.

—Amirul-Mominin Mullah Mohammad
Omer Mujahed

—Mofti Mohammad Masoom Afghani
Acting Minister of Public Health

APPENDIX C

NOTE: The following document is an appendix to the *Final report on the situation of human rights in Afghanistan,* GENERAL E/CN.4/1997/59 (February 20, 1997), submitted by Mr. Choong Hyun Paik, Special Rapporteur, in accordance with Commission on Human Rights resolution 1996/75., as it appears in the web site: www.reliefweb.int

Economic and Social Council Distr. GENERAL E/CN.4/1997/59
20 February 1997 Original: ENGLISH

COMMISSION ON HUMAN RIGHTS
Fifty-third session
Item 10 of the provisional agenda
Question of the Violation of Human Rights and Fundamental Freedoms In Any Part of the World, with Particular Reference to Colonial and Other Dependent Countries and Territories

Final report on the situation of human rights in Afghanistan submitted by Mr. Choong-Hyun Paik, Special Rapporteur, in accordance with Commission on Human Rights resolution 1996/75

Islamic State of Afghanistan
General Presidency of Amr Bil Marof Wa Nai Az Munkir
(religious police)
Administration Department

To: The received letter from the Cultural and Social Affairs Department of General Presidency of Islamic State of Afghanistan No. 6240 dated 26.09.1375 [December 16, 1996] states that:
The role and regulation of Amr Bil Marof Wa Nai Az Munkir is to be distributed via your office to all whom it may concern for implementation.

1. To prevent sedition and uncovered females (be hejab): No drivers are allowed to pick up females who are using Iranian burqa. In the case of violation the driver will be imprisoned. If such kinds of female are observed in the street, their houses will be found and their

husbands punished. If the women use stimulating and attractive cloth and there is no close male relative with them, the drivers should not pick them up.

2. To prevent music: To be broadcasted by the public information resources. In shops, hotels, vehicles and rickshaws cassettes and music are prohibited. This matter should be monitored within five days. If any music cassette is found in a shop, the shopkeeper should be imprisoned and the shop locked. If five people guarantee, the shop could be opened and the criminal released later. If a cassette is found in a vehicle, the vehicle and the driver will be imprisoned. If five people guarantee, the vehicle will be released and the criminal released later.

3. To prevent beard shaving and its cutting: To be broadcasted by the public information resources. After one and a half months if any one is observed who has shaved and/or cut his beard, he should be arrested and imprisoned until his beard gets bushy.

4. To prevent not praying and order gathering prayer at the bazaar: To be broadcasted by the public information resources that the prayers should be done on their due times in all districts. The exact prayer time will be announced by the Amr Bil Marof Wa Nai Az Munkir department. Fifteen minutes prior to prayer time the front of the mosque, where the water facilities and possibilities are available, should be blocked and transportation should be strictly prohibited and all people are obliged to go to the mosque. At the prayer time this matter should be monitored. If young people are seen in the shops they will be immediately imprisoned. If five people guarantee, the person should be released, otherwise the criminal will be imprisoned for ten days.

5. To prevent keeping pigeons and playing with birds: To be broadcasted by the public information resources that within ten days this habit/hobby should stop. After ten days this matter should be monitored and the pigeons and any other playing birds should be killed.

6. To eradicate the use of addiction and its users: Addicts should be imprisoned and investigation made to find the supplier and the shop. The shop should be locked and both criminals (the owner and the user) should be imprisoned and punished.

7. To prevent kite flying: First should be broadcasted by the public information resources advising the people of its useless consequences such as betting, death of children and their deprivation from education. The kite shops in the city should be abolished.

8. To prevent idolatry: To be broadcasted by the public information resources that in vehicles, shops, room, hotels and any other places

pictures/portraits should be abolished. The monitors should tear up all pictures in the above places. This matter should be announced to all transport representatives. The vehicle will be stopped if any idol is found in the vehicle.

9. To prevent gambling: In collaboration with the security police the main centres should be found and the gamblers imprisoned for one month.

10. To prevent British and American hairstyles: To be broadcasted by the public information resources that people with long hair should be arrested and taken to the Amr Bil Marof Wa Nai Az Munkir department to shave their hair. The criminal has to pay the barber.

11. To prevent interest charges on loans, charges on changing small denomination notes and charges on money orders: All money exchangers should be informed that the above three types of exchanging money are prohibited in Islam. In the case of violation the criminal will be imprisoned for a long time.

12. To prevent washing clothes by young ladies along the water streams in the city: It should be announced in all mosques and the matter should monitored. Violator ladies should be picked up with respectful Islamic manner, taken to their houses and their husbands severely punished.

13. To prevent music and dances in wedding parties: To be broadcasted by the public information resources that the above two things should be prevented. In the case of violation the head of the family will be arrested and punished.

14. To prevent the playing of music drums: First the prohibition of this action to be announced to the people. If anybody does this then the religious elders can decide about it.

15. To prevent sewing ladies' cloth and taking female body measures by tailors: If women or fashion magazines are seen in the shop the tailor should be imprisoned.

16. To prevent sorcery: All the related books should be burnt and the magician should be imprisoned until his repentance.

The above issues are stated and you are requested, according to your job responsibilities, to implement and inform your related organizations and units.

Regards,
Mawlavi Enayatullah Baligh
Deputy Minister
General Presidency of Amr Bil Marof Wa Nai Az Munkir